INTO THE GARDEN

Lessons on a Spiritual Journey

Cathy Lynn Gregory

INTO THE GARDEN

Copyright © 2020 by Cathy L. Harmon Gregory

Lord of the Dance words by Sydney Carter
Copyright © 1963 Stainer & Bell, Ltd. (Admin: Hope Publishing Company, Carol Stream, IL 60188) All rights reserved. Used by permission.

Printed in the United States of America

ISBN: 978-1-7349333-0-7

to Kristi Martin and Cindy Whittaker

FOREWORD

I imagine that I'm sitting next to my wife, Cathy Gregory, at her home in East Texas. The warm early summer day cools as we watch the sun slide down toward the horizon. To our right, the garden reveals the earlier plantings, some more mature than others. To our left is the newly mown lawn; its fragrance mixes with that of the flowers planted around us. Where past and present meet, Cathy recounts how she began to write and how her homestead inspired her writings while she lived here, gardened the several beds, raised her children, worked in her antique business, and lived in the midst of God's creation. Here is where her "spirit guide" spoke to her through nature in a way that also accorded with the Christian scriptures.

I taught religious studies for 25 years at Radford University in Virginia, and I encouraged students not only to understand religion academically, but also to view their own ideas about religion and religious experience. Cathy's book is what I would call an autobiographical pilgrimage, for we find here important markers in her spiritual growth.

I sense that her journey grew out of her love for gardening and her responsiveness to God. I also claim that this book could be seen as "views" from that pilgrimage which reveals the impact of God on her at different junctures in her life.

Think about what we know about Jesus. We have in the gospel, events and episodes in His life, not a detailed history. The details of Jesus' life become life-changing not only for us who follow Him, but also to the world that has been so influenced by Him. In the same way, as we travel along with the Jesus of the gospels, we travel alongside Cathy in her book as a companion, as she relates the moments that brought God close to her and her close to God. Her own stories are told masterfully, as we are invited to share each event in her life. Her book invites us to be reflective and attentive to God's voice in our own experience, in the Christian Scripture, and in our faith community. You can read it from front to back, or you can read it in regard to your own pilgrimage by skipping through the book and reading the parts that speak to directly to your heart.

As one who does exegesis or studying scripture for its rich meaning, I was interested in the use of the Bible in these lessons. Of course, the main structure of this book consists of Ecclesiastes 3:1-8. Beyond that, passages from the Bible serve several different purposes. Sometimes they serve as the theme for the following exposition. Other times, they underscore the sentiment or the idea that is being explored. Overall their use is very novel; I would label Cathy's use of scripture as experientially driven and literarily rooted. She creates a symbiotic relationship between what she has experienced and observed and the scripture that she employs.

In addition, the scripture that she provides leaps out to engage the reader so that they experience the scripture as a challenge to or a support of their own spiritual journey. This use of scripture is the signature of one who takes seriously the Bible and its role in the life of the Christian.

I recommend Into the Garden, for it reminds me of those who have written the classics. Although those persons, men and women, did write theological or more discursive works, what really stood out in their writings was the personal approach when they spoke of the rigors of the religious life, and living that life in the world while not being of the world. This is a book that relates one person's spiritual journey in order to call others to their own. That is a pure gift.

Russell Gregory, Ph.D.
Emeritus Professor of Religious Studies
Radford University

Help us to be ever faithful gardeners of the spirit, who know that without darkness nothing comes to birth, and without light nothing flowers.

MAY SARTON

ACKNOWLEDGEMENTS

I had no idea when I began writing twenty years ago that the lessons I've learned from God would turn into a book. My good friends, Marie Aughtry and Cindy Whittaker, with whom I shared my journals, encouraged me to keep writing, so, I did. Without the encouragement of these two women, this book may never have materialized. Marie, who is a saint in her own right, helped critique the content of my first manuscript. And Cindy, a strong advocate for my spiritual writings and liturgical dance, like an angelic butterfly, left our world too soon and migrated to heaven.

I must also thank Fr. Gary and David Gish, who, though they may not know, had a profound impact on my spiritual life at a time when I needed it. Fr. Gary, a wellspring of spiritual anecdotes which I still quote today, left an indelible impression on my spiritual life. And David, my praise band director, taught me how to be faithful and optimistic, no matter what ministry I undertook. I must mention also my good friend and African soul-sister, Beatrice, who keeps me grounded in God's Word and spends delightful hours discussing our Lord, scripture, and the world at great length with me. I am indebted to her example of courage and faithfulness.

I believe God places people in our lives at a time when we most need them, and Chilia Martin is one of those people. Because of her spiritual character, attentive care, and intelligent advice, I couldn't have made it through the last three years without her. Lee Self, another friend sent by God, worked through impossible odds to become a Hospice Chaplain, and by doing so, taught me that you are never too old to succeed when you put your heart and mind to it.

Also, I thank my Creekwood Christian Church family in Flower Mound, Texas, who support my dance ministry, as well as my Creekwood women's Bible study group, who I have become indebted to for their loving prayers and kindness during a traumatic time in my life. (Yes, you all get a free copy of my book!)

A special thanks to my daughter, Elizabeth, and son, Spencer, who keep me on my toes with their inexhaustible intelligence and most especially to my dearest husband, Russell Gregory for helping me with his expertise on grammar and theological matters. Finally, thanks to Andria Flores, my editor, who knows how to make a novice writer feel good about herself. Without her support and encouragement, my writings would still be languishing on my computer.

CONTENTS

INTRODUCTION:

INTO THE GARDEN

Lessons on a Spiritual Journey

As far back as I can remember, I have scribbled poems and random thoughts in dime- store journals and on scrap bits of paper. When poems or thoughts spontaneously revealed themselves to me, I wrote them down. Some of my earliest writings depicted my struggles through a difficult childhood. Poems would meander aimlessly inside my head, so I swiftly wrote them down, without thought of composition or grammar, for fear their content would be lost. When I turned eighteen, my best friends and I traveled through Europe. I carried a journal with me to keep account

1

of my experiences. Its jumbled contents reflected my thoughts and inner-most feelings.

Later in life, I commenced writing in the early stages of my first marriage. I found it cathartic to journal all of my hopes, fears, and feelings. For whatever reason, I hoarded these memoirs in shoe boxes and hid them in my closet. Years later, I rediscovered these accounts containing bits of myself that had long been buried.

Each memoir delightfully revealed to me my love of nature and gardening, a gift I inherited from my Mother. Reading these forgotten texts opened my mind's eye, and I imagined my childhood home with a modest backyard where I used to play. I remembered rusted wheelbarrows mounded with juicy red strawberries, sweet pea tendrils climbing painted wooden fences, and an old gray wagon that used to serve my sisters and I, like we were pioneers in a make-believe western world.

I remembered my favorite book, *The Secret Garden*, a story about Mary Lennox, a young girl in England who, when transported to her rich uncle's castle, discovers a hidden garden abandoned by its caretakers. Mary not only uncovered the beauty of the love that once filled the garden, but through the magic of the garden, befriended her sickly cousin and helped him heal again. Something magical struck me about that story, and I wished for a secret garden of my own to retreat to in times of trouble.

It is no surprise that years later, with borrowed money and a few prayers, I purchased my first home in the black lands of East Texas. I hoped to create a secret garden just like Mary's. My one-acre field, barren and neglected, had barely enough nutrients to enable an aging elm tree to survive. Over the years, through toil, sweat, and prayer, I amended the soil, planted a variety of trees, several antique roses, and clusters of mixed perennials.

This humble acre became a sacred place for me. I toiled, sweated, planted, and harvested, but mostly spent quiet time contemplating my life and praying about the circumstances I had suffered and difficulties I needed to overcome. I spoke to God and questioned His sanity over the trials and tribulations He had allowed me to endure in my life. I cursed, raged, laughed, and cried. And because of my fervor, I suppose, God began speaking to me. He pointed out incredible parallels between our hearts' hidden messages and the lessons of gardening. God would teach me about pain and suffering, as well as love and grace. To the best of my ability, I began to record all that He told me and wove it into the narrative of the following essays.

I started writing this memoir fifteen years ago when I first began hearing Jesus, God, or the Holy Spirit, speaking to me. I often refer to this voice in my mind as my "spirit guide" for the things I hear (and sometimes it comes in so fast, I can't write it down) are profoundly simple and true. I have come to believe that God speaks to us in our own language. I am practical, simple, and down to earth, and don't engage in fantasy or wild notions. Direct in my speech, I call things the way I see them, (sometimes without a lot of tact.) The

CHAPTER 1

"A Time to be Born"

He who is not busy being born
Is busy dying.

BOB DYLAN

LESSON 1

In the Beginning

The Garden of Eden is where it all began, man and woman dwelling amongst an array of trees, roses, birds, butterflies, and bees dancing in the dappled sunlight. Cocooned in Paradise, Adam and Eve were protected by their loving God, as long as they obeyed His direction.

I have often wondered why God chose the Garden as the beginning of life. Why did He place his favorite creation there? I imagine God wanted to protect them by creating a paradise they would never want to leave, similar to the way parents try to keep their children safe in their homes by shielding them from the reality of the harsh world. Like innocent children, Adam and Eve were not aware of the cruel environment outside the life of the Garden. Eventually however, the Tempter entered and proved too great a trickster for their mortal souls. Soon Adam and Eve suffered the hard lessons of their choices and were cast out of the garden. They foolishly made their decision without consulting their Creator. Prior to eating the forbidden fruit, they weren't even aware of their own nakedness (Gen. 2:25); they had no shame.

When my children were toddlers, we enjoyed the

nightly ritual of the "naked-run." After their baths, they romped through the house while we chased them. They giggled and squealed as their squatty legs ran as fast as they could move! Without fearing judgement, their freedom of expression revealed their sweet naivety, which is one of the many endearing qualities of children. They had no shame of their nakedness. But like Adam and Eve, all children must grow up and learn about life beyond the safety of their home. They must learn how fragile their innocence is and how easily it can be lost. When they no longer have the security of their parents' protection, they must learn through their own actions that life's choices come with consequences.

After eating the fruit of the knowledge of good and evil (Gen. 2:17), Adam and Eve's actions revealed that temptation and evil exists in the world. Their consciousness came into being when they rebelled against God. They were exposed and felt shame. Their journey, much like ours, began when they fell from grace. Like children who go astray, we make choices every day that cast us into dark places. When we find our way back to the love and protection of our Creator, we return to grace. And when we do, like the prodigal son, we are welcomed with open arms!

CHAPTER 2

"A Time to Die"

Worry never robs tomorrow of its sorrow,
It only saps today of its strength.

A.J. CRONIN

LESSON 1

Fear and Worry

As a little girl, I was fearful and worried. I didn't know about God and His loving ways. I was apprehensive about the unknown and feared the rejection, judgement, and anger of my parents. And if that was not enough, I feared heights, doctors, dogs, and crowds of people. I tried to overcome my fears by wearing a mask of courage and laughing a lot. On the exterior, I seemed like a happy-go-lucky child, but internally I suffered anxieties. My mother viewed feelings as weak. So, fearing her rejection, I turned inward and hid my fears. Both my parents doubted the existence of a loving God because they had no faith to lean on. They didn't know how to show love because they didn't know about the love of God who teaches us to love unconditionally. They were closed off to the idea of surrendering to a higher power and were filled with the weeds of anxiety, depression, and anger. Sadly, I believe they had no one to love or comfort them either.

God tells us in 1 John 4:18 "There is no fear in love: but perfect love casts out fear..." (NASB) Love and trust in God help us co-create peace. By trusting Jesus as the "weed-eater" of our souls we demonstrate faith in His power and find courage to move through the debris of our fears and into the light of love. "Take courage! It is I. Don't be afraid." Matthew 14:27 (NIV) As we learn from scripture, Jesus is near when we fear. When we falter in our faith, or let our imaginations run wild with apprehension, Jesus frees us by releasing our worries and letting us know that no matter what we are going through, it's going to be okay because He is with us. No longer drowning in fear, we can experience joy and comfort because He is there to guide us through the rough waters of fear we are facing. By taking up the cross and following God, we are blessed to live and grow in the illuminating light of His love rather than fear. We are blessed to become agents of peace in our own life and relationships.

When fear and worry consume our minds, they leave little room for the light of God to enter in. With energy drained, we tend to view life circumstances from a worst-case-scenario and lose hope. By obsessing over worries and fears, our minds become overrun with anxiety and choke out our peaceful state of being. In this state of fear and worry, we are unable to experience God's wonderous gifts of love, compassion, hope, forgiveness, and peace.

Faith, above all, energizes and magnifies, where fear and worry paralyze and cripple. Faith brings us together in love and compassion, where fear separates and divides. Faith draws us closer to God and gives us the courage to face our fears with relentless perseverance. Fear moves us away from our Creator and into darkness, where we suffer in solitude and despair. When we've faltered in the midst of fear and found faith, we've journeyed with God because through the dark tunnel of fear, He lights the way, and by doing so, darkness is transformed into light. Just as Jesus' death became joy with the resurrection, God's presence turns every darkness to light.

By living in His light, we can be sure we are resting in peace rather than the turmoil of fear or worry. "So do not fear, for I am with you..." Isaiah 41:10 (NIV)

When a parent consoles a child who is afraid of monsters under the bed, the parent says, "Do not fear, I am with you." God speaks to us the same way. When we trust Him as a child trusts a parent, we are relived of our anxieties. But only in trust and belief may our fears be comforted and soothed. Our worry worn minds let us know that we are not trusting God enough to steer the boat. James 1:6 states "But when you ask, you must believe and not doubt, because the one who doubts is like a wave of the sea, blown and tossed by the wind." (NIV)

By trusting and listening to God in fearful moments, we can be sure he will direct us. Joshua 1:9 says, "Have I not commanded you? Be strong and courageous. Do not be afraid; do not be discouraged, for the Lord your God will be with you wherever you go."(NIV) Jesus reassures us that when we live in the kingdom of God's love, we have nothing to fear because fear is the opposite of Love. Love cannot fear, and fear cannot love. Perfect love casts out fear, and when we love one another, love ourselves, and love God, fear evaporates. Faith and love leads us through the darkest hour of our need and His word will guide and counsel us along the way. We are never alone because He will not forsake us. Whether or not we have been perfected in love makes no difference to God; He accepts us for who we are and what we are in the moment. He loves us unconditionally, and when we love and surrender to Him with our whole heart, trusting in His word, fears and worries wash away, and faith and love reside.

CHAPTER 3

"A Time to Plant"

*Even if I knew that tomorrow the world
would go to pieces
I would still plant my apple tree.*

MARTIN LUTHER

LESSON 1

Preparing

When I planted my garden years ago, I hurried happily to the nursery to purchase a variety of flowers and shrubs that would adorn my humble home. I dug holes, stuck them in the ground, and sadly watched them die after the first drought of summer. Because I neglected to properly prepare the soil to protect the tender plants from difficult weather conditions, my efforts failed. I had not developed a master plan for watering or keeping weeds at bay. Through this humbling experience, I discovered that the most important time in the garden are the days I spend in preparation. As I tilled, weeded, and amended the soil with manure, I contemplated this idea of "soil versus soul," and God led me to the necessity of preparing my heart and mind to receive His word.

Now I am not suggesting that we add manure to our diets (that's a topic for another day). What I am saying, essentially, is our soul, when properly prepared with God's Word, will thrive no matter the harsh or difficult times we face.

> *"...Prepare Ye The Way of the Lord..."*
> **ISAIAH 40:3 (KJV)**

The conditions that severely damage our spiritual union with God can be avoided through the preparation of prayerful meditation, and study. As we read and meditate on God's Word and tend to our souls with prayers of thanksgiving, repentance, and supplication, we nourish not only ourselves, but others who may be struggling through difficult times. The preparation of prayer and study nourishes us with spiritual food that provides sustenance for our transformation into heavenly beings. As we develop into Christ-like beings, we become like trees protecting and nourishing fragile flowers beneath. As spiritual symbols of nourishment, transformation, union, and fertility; trees represent both growth and resurrection, two necessary dimensions of the spiritual life.

As perfect examples of how to live, grow, transition, change, and even die, trees teach us much about preparation and life. Have you ever looked at the rings on a trunk of a tree? Each ring represents one year, marking a historical timeline of the tree's life. During drought, trees suffer, and roots are forced deeper into the earth to search for needed water. During times of great distress, humans are forced to dig deeper into their spiritual selves and often discover the meaning and purpose of God within. Without suffering, like the trees, we would be shallow and emotionally topple when confronted with difficulties. Suffering then becomes part of the preparation for the eternal life to come. With deeper roots, our lives are enriched because we have endured hardships without falling into sin and despair.

Sometimes we have to endure the same types of suffering over and over because we haven't learned the spiritual lessons needed in the challenges we face. We haven't prepared our hearts and minds with the nourishing and sustaining Word of God. Although we cannot foresee every event of suffering, we can count on our daily habits of connection with God to help us endure. When we open our eyes to see suffering as a necessary gift, we begin to develop healthy spiritual roots, and understand the need for preparation as necessary to our growth.

Preparing our souls helps to strengthen us, guide us, and teach us that God will protect our heart, soul, and mind from the forces of evil when they come. In the midst of the storm, His reassurance calms our minds and brings us peace where otherwise we would be engulfed by fears and fall prey to despair. Sublime peace, whether in suffering or good times, happens when we have prepared our hearts and minds to receive God's word. Ephesians 6:15 talks about the need to "...shod our feet with the preparation of the gospel of peace." (NASB) Preparing to walk on a journey with God means being fitted with readiness.

In gardening, wisdom advises, "a fifty-cent plant into a fifty-dollar hole." A plant can only survive when we spend time and money preparing and enriching the soil in which we place it. When we spend time nourishing our spirituality with God's Word, our lives begin to grow in the light and grace of God. Our soul's soil, when prepared properly, becomes enriched with love, laughter, peace, and joy.

Preparation does not eliminate suffering in this life, but it does strengthen and enrich us in ways we could never imagine. Without preparation we, like sheep, would be lost in the chaos of a sin-filled world. Preparation of our souls helps us develop spiritual roots which minimize the chaos and allows us to sustain with grace and peace the earthly storms when they arrive.

God prepares a place for us to walk with Him in His heavenly garden. He has been planning it for a very long time. Our path is to walk with Him every day, preparing for the eternal journey. Our lives, like a garden, flourish when we spend time preparing. As we prepare the way, God holds our heart and hand, guiding and protecting us on our journey. He sees us through stormy days and revels in gladness as we conquer the sin-filled world in which we are a part. In preparation we may anticipate with joy, a life in Christ and the life ever after.

> *"And if I go and prepare a place for you. I will come again, and receive you unto Myself, that where I am, there ye may be also."*
>
> JOHN 14:3 (KJV)

LESSON 2

God's Word

Like the sun breaking through the clouds illuminating a glorious garden, the light of God's Word enriches our lives and allows us to see clearly the path on which we are to embark in a fallen world. Not only does God's Word light our path, it also gives us a firm foundation to build our spiritual house on. God tells us that if we live by His Word, our spiritual foundation will be like a solid rock because faith stands firm in the face of trials and tribulations. God's prophet Isaiah proclaimed that even as the world fades and passes away, God's Word will remain eternal. (Isa.40:8)

God's eternal Word comes to light when we study and meditate on scripture. His radiant nature is revealed to us in unexpected and exciting ways, and we are blessed to witness His power at work in our lives. As we study scripture, truth is revealed when we open our hearts to see and hear through our spiritual senses all He has to say. The wisdom of God's Word brings clarity to issues that we don't see through the lens of our human perspective. Often this clarity emerges in a sudden awareness when we are not studying, but rather in an "aha" moment where something that was unclear to us becomes very clear. God's Word brings spiritual truth, and that truth manifests in our hearts through study of His word; it takes root, and we begin to grow spiritually. However, if we lose sight of God's Word and become subject to deceit or the distractions of the world in which we live, we become vulnerable to the manipulative ways of the dark side. An example of this is the story of Adam and Eve, where even though God had given clear instruction of what they could and could not do, the serpent manipulated them with deceitful and tempting words.

" *...no lie is of the truth.* "
1 JOHN 2:21 (KJV)

The serpent deceptively told them what they wanted to hear in order to tap into their human desires. These human desires or worldly distractions block our spiritual growth today just as much as they did back then. The fallen world convinces us through commercialism and consumption that true happiness lies in material rather than spiritual things. These earthly lies come disguised in many forms, and if we are not bathed in the light of God's Truth, like Adam and Eve, we become targets of the darkness of deceit.

Not only does our culture deceive us, but God's Truth can be easily perverted by well-meaning scholars and religious leaders. Jesus knew this, so He asked his disciples "...Who do you say I am?" Mark 8:29 (NIV) In that way Jesus was asking them to individually seek truth and not rely solely on collective or corporate doctrines. This concept of an individual relationship with Christ is important because God wants both an individual, as well as a collective relationship with us. *Logos* and *Rhema* are two Greek words that explain this. *Logos* means the study of scripture and *Rhema*, a lesser known word, refers to the personal relationship with Christ. Both are important to knowing the truth and light of God. The truth to many individuals may be that Jesus plays different roles in their lives. He may be a teacher, healer, father, or friend, as well as Lord and Savior. Corporately however, we worship according to the doctrines set forth by each denomination, which may or may not interpret the word of God in the true spirit in which it was given. Because our earthly grasp of God's Word will always be limited by the mere fact that we are fallible human beings our lens of understanding is distorted by our fallen nature. Spiritual growth then, ultimately comes from knowing God both through the experience of our faith in Him along with studying His Word. We must experience the action of faith to know the mystery of God.

Often Jesus strongly chastised the Pharisees who were limited in their *Rhema* relationship with God. They insisted on following their rigid doctrines, rather than seeking the heart of Jewish law. Jesus called them vipers and hypocrites and compared them to yeast, a fungus that can easily get out of control. These are strong words, yet Jesus rightly pointed out they were misusing and misinterpreting God's words to set up rigid laws that benefited them and harmed others.

As the spirit of truth and light of God's Word takes root in us, it reveals God's faithful nature and devotion to our needs. In that way, God's Word becomes paramount to our daily lives. Whether lost, troubled, fearful, or sick, God's words guide, protect, and heal us. For some who have been orphaned, neglected, or abandoned, God's Word is the only truth they know. It is not enough however to just know God's Word. God calls us to be greater than our earthly selves by practicing the virtues necessary for a world that reflects His loving and faithful nature.

> *"Finally, brothers and sisters,*
> *whatever is true, whatever is noble,*
> *whatever is right, whatever is pure,*
> *whatever is lovely, whatever is*
> *admirable—if anything is excellent or*
> *praiseworthy—think about such things."*
>
> **PHILIPPIANS 4:8 (NIV)**

To be noble, pure, lovely, excellent, and praiseworthy in this life is not an easy road to travel. However, as we increase the study of God's Word, our spiritual wisdom and knowledge increases, and our eyes and ears open to what God calls us to be. Spiritual awareness, such as this, requires commitment, faith, and an open heart— commitment of time to spend with God's Word, faith to believe, and an open heart to receive. Through study, we learn that God's Word surpasses our earthly understanding because the spiritual truth and wisdom of God's Word tells us the heart is the home where God resides, and His truth is based on spiritual love, rather than rigid rules.

LESSON 3

Tending the Seed

If we closely examine a seed packet purchased from the nursery, we will see a picture on the packet which illustrates what the seed will grow to look like. The package gives detailed instructions telling the gardener when to plant, how much to water, and whether or not the plant needs sunlight or shade.

Unfortunately, we do not come with instructions printed on our back side, but God knows each of us, and what we need in order to grow into His likeness. As the Master Gardener of our souls, God planted His seed in us, and instructs us to cultivate it with study, prayer, faith, and forgiveness. By doing so, the seed, being fed with the Word of God, has the capacity to manifest into its truest divine form. Like the variety of plants in our garden, each seed's unique form needs individual attention in order to grow wholly. For example, one of us may inherit the seed of compassion and another the seed of courage. When we tend to and nurture these with attention and care, we magnify the Lord, who propagated, scattered, and bound our seeds together in love, so we may do greater things than Christ! (John 14:12) Imagine, if you will, the number of people planted with the seed of God, then imagine those seeds fully grown, multiplying the possibilities of doing greater things than Christ!

We, like Jesus, tend to our seed best by remaining close to the source of our being. If we stray too far, our seed may be strangled by the weeds of temptation and wither under its hold. In Matthew 13:4-8 Jesus tells the parable of the sower and the seed. He talks about worldly things that inhibit the growth of our seed through the metaphor of nature. Ultimately, He claims that the seed grown in good soil produces goodness and truth in spiritual abundance. Worldly things, He explains, represent distractions of our souls, which choke and smother our seed and distance us from the love of God. The power we possess over worldly darkness is to develop deep spiritual roots by remaining close to our Protector through the study of scripture. Studying God's Word encourages us to grow into mature, divine beings by giving us a guidebook to live faithfully in a fallen world. Daily prayer and meditation keep us in constant communication with God, so we worry less, live simply, and love more. Staying close and bringing forth our prayers and petitions before God not only prepares our hearts for His response but unburdens our souls of unnecessary worries and fears. Forgiveness helps clear the debris that lingers from our past, and faith paves the way for a fruitful tomorrow.

When we remain close to God and nurture our seed with study, prayer, faith, and forgiveness, the Master Gardner uproots our earthly weeds and waters us daily with love and grace. He places us in settings where we find companionship with other spiritual beings who help our seed flourish. We are not meant to be alone on the spiritual path, so what we do and with whom we spend our time matters. *Proverbs* 13:20 tells us: "Walk with the wise and become wise, for a companion of fools suffers harm." (NIV) The seed of our divine spirit grows best when we depend on faithful, loving family, friends, and neighbors to provide encouragement, understanding, and support when we need it. Healthy spiritual relationships provide a means to study together, pray together, and to accept each other without judgement. They also keep us from straying into darkness by challenging us in loving ways. God does not mean for us to be entirely independent, rather He wants us to be as children, trusting and dependent on Him for all our provisions. By supplying a spiritual network of other Saints, God ensures we will not fall prey to the weeds of selfish, self-sustaining pride, a spiritual disease of the soul's "soil."

The seed that God planted in us takes a lifetime to mature and blossom. When nurtured with study, prayer, faith, and forgiveness our seed blooms into the likeness of our Divine Creator. While we are growing, we are blessed with the capacity to share our heavenly seed with others who are just beginning to grow. In this way, our life becomes God's legacy, which is passed from generation to generation. When we die, if we're lucky, we may watch with wonder and delight, the young seedlings we nurtured on earth, grow into heavenly beings.

LESSON 4

Patience

My struggle with patience has been life-long. Because of my goal-oriented, type-A personality, I succumb to the call of the Nike commercial: "Just do it!" I don't like to waste time, and my patience evaporates quickly as I fixate on my earthly ambitions. Whether it's filling a grocery list or redecorating an old bathroom, my need for instant gratification in accomplishing my goals supersedes my patience in getting there, and I become frustrated and angry. Webster's Dictionary describes *patience* as *calm endurance*. This conjures up an image of a marathon runner, rather than a sprinter. If you live long enough, spiritual growth becomes a marathon with no end, and patience is one of the keys to reaching the divine "un-finish-line."

At one time or another we get caught in the patience-trap of waiting. Whether waiting for change, a promotion, or a fearful diagnosis, we are filled with anxiety, and our patience grows thin. Fear and frustration take over, and we become anxious and often forget to glean the little moments of joy that God presents to us along the way.

In the garden, patience is acquired through the

laboring task of planning, digging, planting, and prayer. As I plan, I envision a garden filled with sturdy trellises arched with fragrant roses, juicy vegetables, and fresh herbs swarming with butterflies. I dig deep so the plants have room to grow. I plant each plant according to instruction, and then I wait and pray. The rest is in God's hand, and I patiently wait as the plants take time to grow.

One of my favorite children's stories, *Frog and Toad*, written by Arnold Lobel, aptly expresses the notion of patience. Two amphibian companions, opposite in demeanor, teach us lessons about ourselves. Frog, an optimist, and Toad, his fearful and anxious friend, embark on many journeys together. In "The Garden Story," Toad decides he is going to plant a garden and he sets about to plant his seeds. After planting, he sits by the garden and waits for his seeds to grow. When the seeds don't grow, he becomes discouraged and complains to Frog about it. Frog advises him to be patient, but Toad cannot. He storms back to the garden and yells at the seeds to "GROW." Still the seeds do not, so he complains again to Frog who tells him he probably frightened the seeds. Feeling bad about this, Toad returns to the garden and starts singing to the seeds, but they still don't grow. Finally, Toad becomes dejected and leaves the garden alone. Upon return, he discovers little green sprouts shooting up everywhere. He rejoices and realizes that all the seeds needed to grow was a little patience.

As the Master Gardener of our souls, God plants seeds of love in our hearts and patiently watches them grow. He nourishes us through His Word and allows us to grow in our own time. When we fix our gaze upon God as the Caretaker of our spiritual garden, we learn to be patient with ourselves and others in the same way He is patient with us. Through prayer, submission, and relinquishment to God's timing, rather than our own, we come to understand that patience is a virtue worth striving for.

Years ago, when I was struggling with patience, my friend told me a joke. It's about the woman who prayed for patience and God answered her by blessing her with four children. My friend was telling me that even though God listens to our requests, He doesn't always answer our prayers in the way we might wish, so to be careful what we pray for. Now, I might argue with God concerning His wisdom of providing four children as an answer to patience, but I must also accept that He knows what's best for me. In patience I've learned to pray, wait dutifully, and rejoice that He will work out His plan according to His time, not mine. This is very difficult for someone like me with little patience. But walking the slow spiritual journey, I've learned, requires patience to master ourselves in obedience to God. In the famous song "You Can't Always Get What You Want," written by Mick Jagger, we learn a valuable lesson. God doesn't always give us what we want but God always gives us what we need.

As we learn to accept God's will and timing over our own, we also learn that the spiritual mastery of patience consists of self-examination, which is the process of unearthing our souls to understand our deepest hopes, dreams, fears, strengths, and weaknesses. With perseverance, practice, and patience, we learn that we, unlike God, are imperfect. We learn that our lack of patience may not be something wrong with others who seem slow and annoying; instead, it may be something in ourselves we are not addressing. Perhaps we need to develop time-management skills, compassion, or less procrastination.

Over the years, in my own self -examination, I've discovered my lack of patience has to do with me believing everything should go as I planned. But as we all know, best laid plans often go awry. For example, if I am in a hurry in a grocery store, the line is going to be long or slow, the cashier dreadfully chatty or incompetent. Or worse yet, the line may be short, and I, feeling smug for securing the shortest line, watch in horror as the customer in front of me pulls out a box full of coupons! In this moment of utter frustration, I have learned to laugh at the situation, as if watching a scene in a movie or sit-com, as it is always easier to laugh at another's frustrations as opposed to our own.

In more dire situations, I have marveled how some people cope with their problems with seemingly effortless patience: the mother who is diagnosed with breast cancer, parents who lose a child, or a man who loses his job and has to find a way to support his family. Could it be that calm endurance is the fruit of their spirit? A client of mine used to tell me, "If everyone had the chance to sit down and trade their problems, they would end up taking home their own." For sure, I would not want to trade my grocery store frustrations for the fear of a devastating diagnosis. Even so, I would like to acquire the divine fruit of patience to help me conquer my frustrating foibles.

Painfully, as I've searched myself, I've fallen woefully short, yet I believe the struggle for patient endurance is worth it. I believe, through practice and prayer, we can master the unmastered and feel good about the results. The calm that comes from patience is worth fighting and praying for. It gives us a sense of victory over the emotional reactivity that occurs in our minds and re-wires our brains to the spiritual center where peace and relatedness reside. Instead of seeing the woman with coupons as frustrating, I can begin to see that perhaps she struggles with finances, and I develop compassion rather than disdain. I can spend my time praying for her and thanking God that I no longer struggle with financial worries.

The Bible calls patience a "fruit of the Spirit" Galatians 5:22 (ESV) along with love, joy, peace, kindness, generosity, faithfulness, gentleness, and self-control. These virtues fill up the garden of God's kingdom, and with patience we can reap what we sow, all the while receiving God's promise as our reward! With patient endurance we can forgive ourselves each time we fall short of our goal. We can examine the root cause of our entitled sense of time and vow not to let it smother the love we have for others or our self. With patience we can decide whether or not something is worth pursuing, and with patience we can end or endure it. With God's help and in God's time we can learn patience and, in so doing, we can spread that good virtue like a pebble rippling through water. I believe the world can use a little more love and patience, and I believe it begins with me.

CHAPTER 4

"A Time to Kill"

No man can serve two masters:
for either he will hate the one and love
the other;
or else he will hold to one and despise
the other.
Ye cannot serve God and Mammon.

MATTHEW 6 KJV

LESSON 1

Temptation

*" ....And lead us not into temptation;
but deliver us from evil.*

LUKE 11:2 (KJV)

The Lord's Prayer acknowledges that we are weak and fallible human beings. It implores God's help to protect us from the lure of temptation and the deception of evil. It gives glory to God's power against the dark forces and asks that His will be done on earth as it is in Heaven. The Lord's Prayer refers to God as Father, symbolizing God's role in our life as Someone who protects, guides, and loves us. Like good parents, God shields us by setting boundaries and asking we be obedient to His Word. He knows the Tempter is deviously clever and attacks our weaknesses in creative and provocative ways to lead us astray. For most of us, temptation starts at around two years old. How many times have we laughed at an adorable two-year-old, who grabs an "off limits" object while innocently smirking at their parents? We think it cute, and it is, but like God, we must protect our children from harm by setting appropriate limits. We must set boundaries because we know from experience the pitfalls of temptation. Mothers and fathers guard their children as best they can, yet still their children can make dangerously wrong choices despite their best efforts.

Adults make bad choices too. God warns us against our thoughts, deeds, and unhealthy desires. He knows the line between temptation and sin is very thin. He invites us to take inventory, assessing our own sins with confession, rather than pointing the critical finger at others. Temptation can easily ensnare us, and we can fall prey to its schemes. When poor choices are made, we hide our shame and isolate ourselves from others. Isolation, however, isn't the answer, as it destroys our well-being because we were not meant to walk this path of temptation alone.

In troubled times, we must call on trusted friends, family, and God to help us overcome our weaknesses. God implores us to acknowledge our shortcomings as well as hidden desires and learn the tricks of the Tempter, who exploits them. While girding ourselves from his slippery schemes, we must learn to live in truth and keep a watchful eye on ourselves, our choices, and our temptations. Temptation is a lifelong battle. It catches us when we are weak and drains us of vital energy and life. Since our parents can no longer protect us, our choice of close friends matters. God tells us to choose our friends wisely. Proverbs 13:20 tells us *"Walk with the wise and become wise, for a companion of fools suffers harm. (NIV)* Choosing wise friends strengthens us against the enemy of our souls. Wise friends, family, and spouses will counsel, nurture, and love us through trials and tribulations. They will treat us with compassion, rather than judgement, and instill hope, instead of fear. Good friends and family who have walked the spiritual path offer wisdom from their experiences.

In sin, we are separated from God because we are deluded into thinking ourselves worthless and unworthy of being loved by God. Or, we may think we are perfect and in total control, while rebuking God as our sovereign power. Both self-sufficiency and lack of self-worth separate us from the love of God because neither trusts the benevolence of our Father who saves us from ourselves so that we may be recreated in His image. When we abide in Christ, we build a fortress of protection by allowing God's wisdom to take root in our souls, strengthen our hearts, and guard against forces which harm or deceive us. This fortress, founded in faith and bound in love, protects and guides us as we travel the journey of faith together. When we embrace Christ, we embrace freedom—freedom from the internal battles of pride, covetousness, lust, anger, greed, envy, and sloth.

Our internal battle with sin shows up as pain. Pain in our relationships, work- places, churches, and homes. It cannot be won without the help of God and others. Often, we attempt to pacify our pain with addictions, diversions, and denial in order to mask the suffering that lies beneath the surface, but these diversions become a temporary fix like a band-aid over a gushing wound.

Like a carny at a circus, sin's desire entices us to soothe our pain with shiny objects or cheap temporary thrills. In our desperate search for relief, we are easily lured into its treacherous trap. Even though short-lived, sin leaves us feeling empty and weak, opening the door to more temptation. Caught on a hamster wheel of sin's destruction, God tells us the only way to break the cycle of sin is to confess and repent. He tells us that by confessing our sins we will be cleansed from all unrighteousness (1 John 1:9) In repentance, God wants to unmask our dark side, exposing it to truth and light. He wants to help restore us from the inside out. Healing begins when we remove our mask and confess our sins.

Evil masks itself in the same way a parasite masks itself as the host plant. Little by little the parasite takes over, and if not kept in check, it demolishes the vitality of its prey until it dies. When we allow the enemy to consume us, we become lifeless and dry. We become anxious, depressed, and disconnected from life. If we want to heal, we must bring our dark thoughts or deeds to the light of God's love and ask for forgiveness. Only through true repentance are we able to be restored to our authentic selves. With God's help, love, and forgiveness, we can live fully the life we were meant to live.

In the divine world there are no masks; each person is accepted fully and without judgement. Our wholeness comes from revealing ourselves to God through repentance and prayer, and by doing so, we are filled with the Holy Spirit. When we learn to laugh at our weaknesses, denounce those things that would tear us apart, and bring light to dark regions of our soul, we expose ourselves to divine light. Through thick layers of darkness, God heals our sins until our divine spirit shines through.

> *"Submit yourselves therefore to God,*
> *resist the devil, and he will flee from you"*
>
> JAMES 4:7 (KJV)

In the face of temptation, having a battle plan protects our hearts and minds from spiritual chaos. The plan includes girding our loins with truth and wearing the breastplate of righteousness. (Ephesians 6:11-20) It includes declaring our weakness before God, which guarantees He will send out a force of angels to help us in our spiritual battle. (Hebrews 1:14)

When we feel darkness engulfing us in work, marriage, or with our children, we must imagine slamming the door to temptation's knock, while inviting God in.

The depths of our divine wholeness depend entirely upon our ability to remain faithful during the trials and temptations we face. By invoking the Lord's Prayer, we ask not to be led into temptation. We ask for forgiveness and the ability to forgive others. Our sins have already been paid through the Deliverer, Who willingly bears the cross of our pain. Through the light of our Redeemer, sin's wounds are healed, and we are restored to wholeness.

CHAPTER 5

"A Time to Heal"

For, lo, the winter is past,
the rain is over and gone;
The flowers appear on the earth;
the time of the singing of birds is come,
And the voice of the turtle is heard in
our land.

SONG OF SOLOMON 2:11-
12 KJV

LESSON 1

Healing

Remember as a child when your favorite toy broke, or you scraped your knee? Bucket-sized tears rolled down your cheeks and left your young heart wounded and raw. In this tender moment of distress, you couldn't ever imagine feeling better, yet, if you were lucky, a kind soul restored your toy, or gently wiped your knee and patched it with a band-aid and some love.

God heals our broken hearts in the same way the kind adult helped us when we were young. Lost in our hurt, we know God feels our pain and suffers with us. When we suffer, God suffers, much like a parent does when their child is sick or in trouble. Although it may not always feel like it, He intuitively knows what we need in order to heal. He offers the balm of grace, love, mercy, forgiveness, comfort, and compassion as much as we are willing to accept them.

Unlike the broken toy, our mending doesn't happen overnight. Healing takes time, and in time, most wounds heal. When our vulnerability overwhelms us, we feel weak and alone. In these moments exposing our weaknesses and fears to the Great Healer proves difficult. We may be unsure of our needs or feel we won't be heard. But rest assured, God knows what we need before we even ask. He asks only our trust and faith that He will take care of us in our time of need. If we submit in this way, we will be wrapped in a blanket of divine comfort and love

We read in John that when Jesus saw the invalid who had not entered the water, he asked, "Do you want to be made well?" John 5:6 (NKJV) The man who had been disabled for many years replied that he was unable to get to the pool because he had no one to help him. Then Jesus said, "Get up! Pick up your mat and walk." John 5:8 (NIV) Instantly the man was cured and walked into the pool. In order to "get up and walk," we must open the door to healing and allow our faith to be crystallized by our belief in the power of Jesus. Our faith in God makes us well. When we are open to the powers of His healing grace, we open ourselves to the light of divine creation that restores us to wholeness. If we are closed, we get caught in dysfunctional "rinse and repeat" patterns which leave us feeling tired and wrung out. These cycles cannot be broken until we realize where we need healing, then ask for God's help where we specifically need it.

The first step toward recovery begins with being at peace with "what is" and asking God to help us accept our condition and trust in whatever He ordains to help us heal. By acknowledging our deepest fears and weaknesses openly, we admit to ourselves that we can't go it alone without help from a higher power. Imbued with the divine spirit of God, we possess the capability to heal ourselves, but first we must acknowledge His spirit within, which manifests as a radiating balm when we access it. True healing then is manifested in spiritual communion with God by remembering Christ who suffered for our sins. As caretaker of our souls, He shows us the way, the truth, and the light. He is everywhere and in everything, so we are wise to stay alert and listen to His still small voice and acknowledge His Holy Spirit dwelling in and among us.

Healing comes in many forms and God teaches us that healthy, loving human connection promotes healing. Connection to others manifests wholeness and health when tended to. In connectedness, we can share the healing grace of God by sharing our healing journey. It is then we start to realize we are not alone, that others have suffered through and made it to the other side of their pain. By sharing the path in which others have traveled, we learn about God's light and love. We learn that walking the healing path with others allows us to celebrate the joys and suffering that come with recovery.

On our spiritual healing journey, we sometimes discover the need for healing our inner- child's woundedness. Sometimes in our need to protect our child's vulnerable self, we hide our spiritual pain under layers of anger, detachment, judgement, or sin. Removing these layers, ultimately becomes part of healing. It's a painful process of submitting whole-heartedly to God's sovereign healing grace, as each layer, like those of an onion, is carefully peeled away. With gentleness and love, God dismantles the ego-child's wounded layers, removing our false self-protections and replacing them with love for God, ourselves, and others. As it was with the invalid, our constant faith in His power becomes paramount to full recovery.

Whether in physical or spiritual crisis, God uses our brokenness to meet and love us exactly where we are. In so doing, we begin to see the light of His merciful healing grace as one of acceptance and love. This grace of acceptance and love forges a path to the heart-center of our divine souls, where His spirit was planted at our birth. As we rediscover His divine spirit within us, we discover our own healing powers as our faith and belief grows.

Central to the ministry of Jesus, healing becomes the hallmark to the pure heart that Jesus possesses. When asked in the fullness of faith, Jesus answered the call to heal without prejudice or need for compensation. As disciples of Christ, we too are granted healing powers in Jesus' name. We are called to maintain purity of heart so that we may serve and heal others without prejudice.

In the fullness of time, He, the Master Creator, intertwines our souls exclusively to His, binding our healing hearts together as one, allowing us to be made whole in His image. When we witness His healing grace, we begin to see the light of His love for all human beings. We begin to see there is no separation between God, Christ, ourselves, and others. Any contrary thought spreads the sickness of disharmony, division, and distrust within us, our world, and God.

When we distance from God or others, we become sick and separated from our Supreme Creator, who in love breathed us into one being. When we come to God and want to be made well, we are submitting the whole of who we are, both good and sinful, and we ask God and others to love us, warts and all. He knows our weaknesses and loves us anyway. He knows our strengths and loves them too. He beckons us to come to the warm comforting womb of His love to be nurtured and healed. As we submit, He protects and guides our inner-child to spiritual and physical wholeness. He embodies us as we embody Him, allowing us to love fully in the unified spirit of His Holy Grace.

In our pain of loss, grief, or physical or mental illness, when we ask for help, we must come to the healing pool of our hearts where we want to be made well and ask God for His healing grace. When we drench ourselves in the healing waters of Jesus, we are soaking up an abundance of love and life and everything good and holy that is rooted in Him. We, in our spiritual drought, beckon God to heal us. In return He asks, "Do you want to be made well?" If so, we must take up the cross of our Redeemer and forge the path less traveled, seeking His guidance, mercy, and healing grace. Thirsty for heaven's gift, we must open wide to receive, and welcome the life sustaining waters of God's love and healing grace.

As I share what I've learned about healing grace, I am reminded of a time years ago when I was selling antiques at a market in Canton, Texas. Late on a

Thursday afternoon, I felt pains in my lower abdomen. Generally, I was stubborn about my health. I didn't trust doctors, so I had learned many natural ways to prevent common illnesses. Mostly, I thought I had eaten something that didn't agree with me. In the course of a few hours, I drank a full bottle of Pepto Bismol and went for a long walk to ease the pain. It didn't work, and the cramping got worse. Thinking I could wait until morning to seek medical attention, I suffered through the night. Around midnight, I rose to use the restroom and passed out. I woke, calling to my husband, who made a few urgent phone calls to find the nearest hospital. When I arrived, I was in the fetal position and sweating profusely. The doctors thought I had an infection of the ovaries and gave me some antibiotics. Throughout the night, I moved in and out of consciousness, the thirst and pain unbearable.

The next morning, the doctor on call ordered a sonogram. As the doctors and surgeons scanned the results, I could hear them whispering in urgent tones. Within an hour I was rushed into surgery. My appendix had ruptured. Although I was conscious of what was taking place, I felt no will to live or die. Headed into surgery, I was rolled down a long corridor. I remember vividly a very large black women standing over my head. She was combing my hair and praying continuously. Her words were soft and whisper-like. I felt comforted. Even in my delirious state, I knew she wasn't part of the staff because I felt her strong spiritual presence. I felt she had been sent from God. The surgery was successful, although I spent eight long days in the hospital and six weeks in recovery. When I went for a follow up, the doctor told me I was considered in the medical profession to be in a "morbid" condition. He said I was lucky to be alive. During my time of healing, my husband had to take over cooking, cleaning, and caring for the children. Until that time, I had done most of those things. For the first time in my life, I had to trust others to care for me. I wondered later if that was God's lesson for me. I wondered why He had sent the black healer-woman. *Why me?* For whatever reason God decided it was not my time to die. I never prayed, nor did I ask to be made well, as the invalid did. Even so, He sent the large black "angel," and she saved me.

LESSON 2

Forgiveness

One cannot speak of forgiveness without talking about sin. Every one of us has sinned, therefore we are all equal in God's eyes. Whether sin is known or unknown makes no difference. Sin can be witnessed in thought, deed, or deed undone. Part of humanness is our sinful nature, so to help us and guide us, God gave Moses the Ten Commandments to be delivered to his people. Whenever I think of the Ten Commandments, I am reminded of Charlton Heston portraying a virile Moses, coming down from the mountain top to deliver God's commandments. In Matthew 5:3-10, we also learn of another venture upon a mountain top where Jesus spoke, proclaiming over one hundred rules in which we are encouraged to live by. Jesus warns that even the least of these violations committed will prevent us from knowing the Father. He tells us His yoke is easy and in order to open the gates to heaven we must repent through private prayer, asking God to forgive us. In return, God promises forgiveness each and every time we break His written laws, not once or twice, but eternally. He also makes clear that if we are to expect to be forgiven, we must first cleanse our own hearts by the act of forgiving others. He warns us not to judge others, for by that same measure we will be judged. *(Matthew 7:1)* I understand most people do not see their own transgressions because they are too busy evaluating others. It is much easier to see what another person is doing right or wrong, than to look at ourselves in the mirror and take account of our own behaviors. Jesus was completely clear on this act of judging others. He said to the people, "Why do you look at the speck of sawdust in your brother's eye and pay no attention to the plank in your own eye?" Matthew 7:3 (NIV) Many times, when we see a behavior in another person that irritates us, it is often an irritating behavior we have that we don't want to see in ourselves.

To observe other people's sinful habits, such as a lack of humility, idle gossip, or laziness, alerts us to a division within ourselves, a division between our own behavior and God's commandments. It signals us to look in the mirror and see ourselves as God sees us, so that we might change. This course involves painful self-examination and a process of feeling guilt and remorse about our past and present sinful behaviors. The distress comes when we see our own transgressions, the pain they've caused, and the inability to know how to stop them.

Forgiveness, therefore, begins with us. In order to change, we must recognize our behaviors, repent, and forgive ourselves as God forgives us. If we learn to accept ourselves, warts and all, it moves us toward change and growth. In so doing, we partake in the divine cycle of forgiveness, whereby God forgives us, we forgive ourselves, and we forgive others. Forgiveness then becomes a spiritual fountain, as it cleanses and restores anger and resentment, and replaces it with peace and love. Forgiveness, however, does not mean allowing others to cross our physical or emotional boundaries. God tells us we must confront offensive behavior with a truthful and loving heart. We can always forgive, but we shouldn't allow certain behaviors to go unchecked.

When I was a teenager, my best friend's parents separated, and she and her sisters went to live with their father. Everyone felt sorry for her because her mother had a difficult personality. She was angry and controlling and flew into rages at the drop of a hat. One afternoon, with tears in her eyes, my best friend confided in me that her father had molested her. She tried to justify what had happened by telling herself that he must not have known what he was doing. Shamefully, she recounted that her body responded in a way that confused her. She did not have the courage to confront him and tried to understand why he would do this unspeakable act. Justifying it in her own mind, she concluded that her father did not get what he needed from her mother. Her father's behavior continued for several years. Each time, she was determined to muster the courage to tell him *no*, but she couldn't. In a way, she confessed, she was testing his love to see if he would stop this sickening behavior on his own. Finally, one day she stood up and angrily shouted at him to stop, and he did.

The guilt and shame she felt for many years haunted her. She became depressed and drank heavily to mask the pain of the abuse. Like a video, she replayed in her mind the immoral scenes over and over again. The guilt, resentment, and anger consumed her; she did not function well in her life. She had no one to turn to for help, so she continued to live with her father's appalling secret until she could no longer bear it.

With nowhere to turn, she decided to pray to God continuously, asking Him to relieve her pain. She heard God telling her that forgiveness was the golden key to release herself from her bondage, to forgive her father for all he had done. She trusted God would not misdirect her. In that moment she bent down on her knees and fully forgave her father for his unspeakable deeds. In her heart, she told me, a serenity swept through her, and she felt peace at last. God had shown her the light of forgiveness, and she was set free. She still loved her father and prayed he would seek professional help. She felt he could have been abused as a child, and that translated into his practice of sin. She forgave herself for her lack of courage, and no longer carries the shame of this event in her heart. As a final gesture, she wrote a letter to her father and explained how his behavior affected her life and how she had forgiven him.

Without forgiveness in our hearts, anger, resentment, guilt, and shame will remain festering wounds in our souls. God has given us the golden key of forgiveness to unlock our hearts, mend our wounds, and repair the damage. As we pray each and every day, we can ask God to cleanse our hearts with forgiveness, so we can feel the light of His love shining through the dark places.

LESSON 3

Relationships

The relationship I have with my garden reflects the relationship I have with God and others. Its ebb and flow mirror the changing seasons and mark the successes and failures inherent in such an endeavor. Whether or not I spend time in my garden, reveals itself come Spring; the tender plants, given proper care and attention will flourish, if neglected they will die. Our relationships are the same. When we spend time nurturing and caring for them, they blossom; when we ignore them, they shrivel. Relationship at its best, seeks spiritual perfection, but does not expect or demand it. In any case, God has placed us with others so that we might learn valuable lessons about ourselves. Those lessons can be hard because relationships can be difficult, and those difficulties may reflect something that needs to change. Ultimately, when we place God above all others, our earthly relationships reflect that divine connection. Who better than our Creator understands the different types of relationships and their complexities? God knows our desires, as well as our weaknesses, and continually points us in the direction of love and acceptance, of ourselves and of others. Love, in all its forms, binds us together and strengthens us in ways we could not achieve alone.

Like plants in our garden, relationship with God and others are either growing or dormant. Slow steady growth is healthy as it allows personal time to deepen our spiritual roots by examining our conscience. Dormant relationships are unhealthy and need to be looked at seriously to determine the cause. If we are spending too much time trying to fix a poor or dormant relationship, or ignoring it altogether, we are not spending enough time developing a relationship with God or ourselves. Whatever type of relationship we are in; honest communication is key. When we communicate honestly with God, ourselves, and others, we open the door to healthy and meaningful connection in all our personal and spiritual interactions. Even though we might not feel close, our loving and truthful communication will sustain the life force of the relationship because truth, spoken in love, is a conscious, loving gesture, which moves us toward peaceful interactions with others.

Sometimes we choose to push the pause button in relationships when peaceful solutions seem unattainable. This is not a bad thing, for when the pause button is pressed, we are given the opportunity to examine ourselves internally, in the light of God's truth. If we are wise, we will take the opportunity to practice humility, empathy, patience, and forgiveness. Before this happens, however, we must release all fears and pre-conceived notions about relationships and allow them to unfold naturally. We cannot force ourselves and our beliefs on others, even if they are good. In some cases, this means accepting the other for who he or she is and letting the relationship go. Not all relationships are meant to last a lifetime. Sometimes, before we make this difficult decision, we must dig up our old hurts, till and amend our minds with healthy thoughts while weeding out sinful habits. This will ensure that future relationships are built on a foundation worthy of God.

Learning to accept others as God accepts us is key to all relationships. We cannot change anyone but ourselves, and truthfully, we cannot change into mature spiritual beings without God. While growing into spiritual maturity, our relationships become more meaningful as we learn to reveal our vulnerabilities honestly, without fear of judgement. Connecting in this way strengthens the spiritual bonds of relationship and mirrors our relationship with God, Who accepts our weaknesses without judgement. There is true healing and humility when we expose ourselves and ask to be forgiven. That being said, revealing our true self to anyone must be done with discernment. Exercising judgement for whom we confide in is crucial, for if we trust the wrong persons, we may end up vulnerable to being wounded again. People who have been wounded in relationship, particularly in a primary one, have trouble confiding in others. They protect their heart by building a fortress around it. Their wounded ego becomes their center, and they protect it mightily. Defensiveness, anger, and false pretense are cover for a sense of shame, loss, and abandonment. These defenses become the walls that separate us from God and others. By blocking others out, we create a sense of loneliness and isolation which may turn into dark fear or depression. When we tear down the walls that keep us from truly knowing and accepting God, ourselves, and others, we return to the intimacy God intended for us in relationship.

> *"Two are better than one, because they have a good reward for their toil. For if they fall, one will lift up his fellow. But woe to him who is alone when he falls and has not another to lift him up! Again, if two lie together, they keep warm, but how can one keep warm alone? And though a man might prevail against one who is alone, two will withstand him-a threefold cord is not quickly broken."*
>
> ECCLESIASTES 4:9-12 (ESV)

In the garden, plants that require the same amount of sunshine and water are grouped together so they may thrive. As humans we are spiritually drawn to others who share a base of values that reflect our own, so it is no accident that God places us with like-minded individuals to help us in our spiritual growth. Ironically, when we see something we don't like in another individual, it may be a reflection of our own hidden self that we don't see. When we begin to see a difference of values in relationship, conflicts arise.

Consequently, if these conflicts are not resolved, they become a wedge of separation and a source of discord. This is when resentment, anger, and mistrust, begin to take root, and if left unchecked, become the weeds that choke our relationships. It is crucial then, to explore differences openly and honestly without judgement. By staying attuned to God and others, we promote a healthy union, where out of love, differences are accepted, and misguided values are challenged. Equally important, we learn to accept, appreciate, and support each other as individuals, while at the same time promoting the growth of the union. Ideally, when we place God at the top of the relationship pyramid, relationships thrive. Sadly, and equally so, when we place ourselves at the top, relationships may perish.

The relationships we have with others are spiritual in nature. How else could we learn about God, ourselves, and others? As we journey through this wonderful terrain, we will encounter many different styles of relationships. *The Four Loves* by C.S. Lewis describes four kinds of human relationships in terms of love: *Storge*, or affection love; *Phileo*, or friendship love; *Eros*, or erotic love; and *Agape*, or divine love. He describes *Storge* love, or affection, as the most-humble type of love, calling it a comfortable kind of love, where two people enjoy each other's company, no matter what they are doing. They have a strong affection for each other and feel good when spending time together. *Phileo*, or friendship love, is when two people share the same interests and goals. The bonding occurs by finding ones who share a love for an interest that they once thought was uniquely theirs. *Eros* is the love that creates the hottest flames and manifests as a bright light or a scorching fire. It seeks one, and only one, passionately. Like being struck by the flaming arrows of cupid, *Eros* love is not a choice and cannot be controlled. Finally, *Agape* is the highest and most unselfish of the loves. It is divine love and goes against our very nature because it seeks to love the unlovable. Charitable and unselfish in nature, this love is the most difficult because it gives all and asks for nothing in return. For this reason, it requires protection of one's heart, in order not to be broken.

No matter the type of relationship we are in, when we cultivate it with God first, we are blessed with the opportunity to be molded into the likeness of the divine, which plays an important role in our relationships. The more we learn to give and sacrifice in our relationships, the more our relationships mirror Jesus, who sacrificed His life for us. Connecting to the divine helps us connect to others. I like to picture in my mind the symbol of the cross, where the longer vertical line reaches toward God, and the shorter horizontal line reaches out to others. We cannot reach out to others if we do not spend more time reaching out to God. Aside from our parents, who may or may not have taught us about healthy relationships, God is our primary source. As Paul wrote, when he considered how the love of God changed his life, "Love is patient, love is kind. It does not envy, it does not boast, it is not proud. It does not dishonor others, it is not self-seeking, it is not easily angered, it keeps no records of wrongs." 1 Corinthians 13:4-5 (NIV)

In life, we may experience many different types of relationships. Those relationships are there for a reason. If we view them as spiritual reflections for learning, our relationships will grow stronger each time we rely on God rather than ourselves to lead them. God guides us toward peaceful interactions with others so we may feel the joy of living in harmony with one another. When our relationships are harmonious, we are filled with the love of our Creator, Who, in order to have a relationship with us, sacrificed His only Son.

Living Waters

In summer when I was young, my parents drove me to the municipal swimming pool. Excited and nervous, I entered the familiar turnstile while listening to the splashing sounds of children in the distance. The recoil of the high dive's spring echoed loudly, and I marveled as each brave soul took the big plunge into the waters below. Somewhat frightened of the large pool, I mustered the courage before stepping into the water. First, I dipped my toes in; if it wasn't too cold, I went up to my ankles, then knees, and finally my upper torso. When I was brave enough, I stretched my arms out wide and swam to the far side of the pool. Even then, I kept my head above water. But finally, I held my breath, submerged, and explored the depths below.

Entering fully into the Living Water of God's Kingdom creates the same exhilaration as testing the waters of a large pool. At first it may be scary because it's an unknown experience, and what we don't know sometimes frightens us. The Living Water of God represents the Word of God, as well as the healing and transforming nature of water. When we are fully immersed in the Living Water, we leap into the depths of an ocean of mercy, grace, and healing in order to be made whole. Many, however, are too frightened or unable to step in and trust the depths of love God has to offer us. But the invitation is clear; in order to be saved, we must enter the water.

John the Baptist stood at the banks of the Jordan River crying out to the people to "...Prepare the way of the Lord and make straight paths for Him" Mark 1: 3 (NIV) He foretold of the coming of a savior and implored the people to come into the water and be baptized. Having invited God's people into the river, John was inviting them into a life with Christ. Along our path, someone may have invited us into the Living Water of Christ. We may have accepted the invitation by attending church once in a while, but shortly thereafter, other things captured our attention, and we were unwilling or unable to attend regularly. Or perhaps we may have entered halfway by exploring God's depth, only to be met with the fear of giving up too much of our selves. This is understandable because taking the full plunge into the Living Water of God's Kingdom is transformational, and change can be scary business, for it requires trust and faith in something unseen and repentance of wrong doings. For these reasons, it is difficult for many to take the leap of faith because unlike a fad, or hobby, taking the plunge, becomes a way of life, and that way of life is rewarding, but not easy.

Like a child who considers the vast depth of a swimming pool before entering, we must consider how much we are willing to trust and believe in the vast depth of something greater than ourselves while examining our conscience. But the joy that comes from making the decision to leap is experienced in our transformation. In the same way water carves mountains out of stone, we become a thing of beauty when shaped by the Living Waters of God's love. There is nothing greater than to feel the depths of God's love that reforms, remakes, and reworks us into the image of Christ, in order to be made whole. "Therefore, if anyone is in Christ, he is a new creation. The old has passed away; behold the new has come." 2 Corinthians 5:17 (ESV)

Not only is water strong enough to carve through rocks over time, water by its very nature is cleansing and therefore healing in nature. In John 5, at the pool of Bethesda, people gathered and waited for the angels to trouble the waters. They believed if they entered while the waters bubbled up, they would be cured of all ailments. When we take the full plunge and believe in the "...spring of the living water,..." Jeremiah 2:13, (NIV) our healing begins. The Living Water of God's Word, cures all that inflicts, whether physical, spiritual, or mental. By plunging into the waters, we swim with the Holy Spirit, and bathe with the angels and saints who transform our souls into divine beings. If we are to be cured of the darkness within, we must want to be made well, accept the invitation, hold our breath, and jump in.

> *"Whoever believes in me, out of his heart*
> *will flow rivers of living water."*

JOHN, 7:38 (ESV)

The Living Waters of God is an eternal well and one which sustains us in everyday life. When we dive deeply into God's Word, we become part of a vast body that allows God's love to flow through us and on to others so they may feel its depths. We become the fountain of Jesus in which others may drink, and a well of eternal wisdom for others to draw from. Our capacity to love others and ourselves, quenches the thirst for all who are seeking a life with more meaning, depth, and purpose. In order to enter and take the exhilarating plunge into the Living Waters, we are called to accept the invitation and have the courage to trust God enough to turn over every aspect of our life to Him so we may be healed and transformed. In so doing, "… whoever drinks of the water that I will give him will never be thirsty again." John 4:14 (ESV)

CHAPTER 6

"A Time to Break Down"

The chains of habit are too weak to be felt
Until they are too strong to be broken

SAMUEL JOHNSON

LESSON 1

Perfectly Imperfect

Growing up as a child, I never got the impression I was okay. It seemed no matter what I did or didn't do, I fell short of my parents' expectations. They criticized more than they praised, and because of that, I felt unsure of myself. I know they were trying to be honest with me, but their honest evaluations became a demand for perfection. Over time, my pursuit of perfection wore down my acceptance of myself, and I struggled with low self-esteem. Thankfully, my life in Christ teaches me I don't have to be perfect in order to be loved. I can be myself, whatever that is, and God loves me regardless. I can strive to be the best I can be without the burden of being perfect. No longer weighed down by the heavy burden of perfectionism, I can rejoice for I am loved, which tells me I am okay whether I fail or succeed. I am "perfectly imperfect" as one of my favorite counselors used to remind me. Even if I don't give my best effort, I can forgive myself and learn to do better next time.

One of the problems with trying to be perfect is that we don't allow ourselves to fail, and failure teaches us much more about ourselves and how we handle disappointments than success does. The good news is,

God not only accepts our imperfections, He uses them to teach others. When we overcome the challenges of our flaws, we witness the example of God's strength and courage by demonstrating that it isn't necessary to be perfect in order to accomplish things of great value. (2 Corinthians 12:9-10) Christ, the Conqueror of doubt and despair, leads us down a path where we accept ourselves and others for who we are, not what we've done or how we've done it. Besides being a problem, perfectionism is annoying, especially when demanded by those who are not perfect. Have you ever witnessed a reformed smoker who chastises others who smoke?

> *"Surely there is not a righteous man on earth who does good and never sins."*
> **ECCLESIASTES 7:20 (ESV)**

People, as well as many religious institutions, place a heavy burden of being perfect or without sin. Perfection, however, cannot be forced through control or manipulative posturing. Humans respond and learn best when another sets a pattern of personal integrity through a loving example. Leading by example works and reaching for the ideal makes us better human beings; if we strive for the stars, we may reach the moon.

> *"You therefore must be perfect, as your heavenly Father is perfect."*
> **MATTHEW 5:48 (ESV)**

Many Christians believe we must be perfect like

God. Striving to be so may be a noble cause, but only in the realization and acceptance that we are imperfect can we come closer to God. Only God is perfect, and the sooner we accept this, the sooner we are on the path to healing. Our imperfections make us human, and through our humanity, we find Christ. We are perfectly imperfect human beings who are wounded in many ways. Christ our Redeemer, rather than being the Savior of the righteous, is the Physician for the weak, wounded, and imperfect. (Luke 5:32)

Interestingly enough, God places us with different people to test our ability to accept one another's imperfections just as He accepts us. In so doing, we often find ourselves faced with the mirror of our own imperfections, which teaches us a great deal about our self. Only by accepting ourselves and others can we begin to grow in the light of God's love and become disciples worthy of His kingdom. In other cases, a common mistake we make is to naively believe a person is whole and perfect and place them on a pedestal where eventually their imperfections emerge, and we judge them harshly for not being "without stain" as we imagined they were.

In a frantic effort to avoid our own flaws, we foolishly become vested in changing others in order to make ourselves feel better. But to force our ideas of perfection on others is a battle we'll lose, for by doing this we are judging another human instead of looking at ourselves. Matthew 7:1-2 wisely says, "Do not judge, or you too will be judged. For in the same way you judge others, you will be judged…" (NIV) Each time we judge another based on our idea of perfection, we are in effect judging ourselves as well. The only way we really connect to perfection, or wholeness of the Divine, is by surrendering to God's way and will. The household I grew up in placed a high value on judging based on superficial perfection, that is, exterior attributes that have no spiritual value. But Jesus says in Matthew 19:21 "If you want to be perfect, go, sell your possessions and give to the poor, and you will have treasure in heaven." (NIV)

Perfectionism in the fallen world is a trap. Our culture spends billions of dollars on facial creams, fancy cars, houses, clothing, Botox, and weight loss diets, to mention a few. Yet, the rate of suicide is up, millions of people are taking anti-depressants, and psychologists are working overtime. Money that could otherwise be spent on something of real value such as helping the less fortunate, is being spent on short-lived products. How many commercials do you see that advocate spiritual fulfillment by looking to God for an example of spiritual perfection?

The path to fulfillment is not forged through being or looking perfect. It begins and ends with faith in something greater than ourselves. Perfection, in the spiritual realm, means to strive to be Christ-like, to walk the path with other imperfect human beings, seeking the perfection of God, Who accepts us as perfectly imperfect. My priest used to say, "People, are just people-ish; they do people-ish things!" I loved this because in a simple way he was saying we are all imperfect, and we must accept it. And by accepting ourselves and others as imperfect, we move in the direction of truth. In truth we learn not to judge others (or ourselves) according to our standard of perfection. Rather, we leave room for error and allow our faith to lead us to integrity and virtue. By patterning after Christ, we teach others by example the greatest two commandments:

> *"'Thou shalt love the Lord thy God with all thy heart, and with all thy soul, and with all thy mind.' This is the first and greatest commandment. And the second is like unto it, '...thou shalt love thy neighbor as thyself.' On these two commandments hang all the law and the prophets.'"*
>
> MATTHEW 22-37 (KJV)

Though unattainable on this earth, striving for spiritual perfection will not be in vain if we keep these two greatest commandments in our hearts. We must remember that through our weaknesses, not our strengths, God uses us for His plan. We do not have to be perfect in order to be loved because God loves our imperfections as much as He loves us.

CHAPTER 7

"A Time to Build Up"

In times of quietness our hearts should be like trees,
Lifting their branches to the sky to draw down strength which they will need to face the storms that will surely come.

TOYOHIKO KAGAWA

LESSON 1

Courage

If individuals possessed the courage when called upon by their divine conscience to do the right thing at the right moment, the world would be a far better place. Fortunately, there are those who, day after day, put themselves on the proverbial line in order to make a difference. They do not take time to ponder or weigh their options for advantage; they listen to their heart and allow God's conscience to be their guide. They see life, not as a mode of personal survival, but as a journey where life takes on meaning of divine proportions. They are willing to fight for causes such as freedom, morality, compassion, and love.

The Bible tells us in Deuteronomy, "Be strong and of good courage..." Deuteronomy 31:6 (NKJV) It tells us that in the face of adversity, we are to stand up for divine principles, even at the risk of our own persecution. In Peter 1 it says, it is better to suffer under righteousness than to suffer because of wrong doing. (1 Peter 3:17) To have courage gives our lives meaning and purpose. It showcases the best of the human spirit and spreads hope to those who live in fear. In the womb of our inner spirit is the seed planted by our

Creator that when nurtured and guided with His love, is waiting to grow into the likeness of Him.

The guiding force of courage helps us to grow into that likeness. It invites us to explore without fear places in ourselves we never knew existed. Whether discovering the artist, poet, humanitarian or activist, courage takes vulnerability to self-actualize into the divine self. As we hunger for reformation into His image, courage strengthens our hearts, fortifies our minds, and arouses our souls. Courage is persevering with determination and finding inner strength in God, Who allows us to overcome incredible obstacles. With Christ at the helm of our spiritual voyage, our shackles of fear are removed, and the bondage of our soul, released. We are able to seek the best of who we are and who we were meant to be because we have the courage to walk with Him in truth and love.

> *"The Lord is my light and my salvation; whom shall I fear?*
> *The Lord is the stronghold of my life; of whom shall I be afraid?"*

PSALM 27:1 (NIV)

The pilgrimage of faith requires courage—courage to stand up to deception, poverty, hunger, rejection, despair, and disease. When we yield to temptation, we yield to darkness and the paralysis of fear. Courage depends on our energizing faith in God, Who longs to strengthen our hearts and bring peace to our souls. In times of tribulation, He doesn't want us to succumb to the paralyzing effects that accompany fear; He wants us to be energized with the faith that whatever we have to face with courage, He will guide and protect us.

Countless times in my life, I've cried out to God to give me strength and courage in my hour of need, and He delivered. When my daughter first began driving, I was a nervous wreck. A typical mom of a teenage driver, I prayed continually for God to protect her, as I had no power to do so. It wasn't long before my worst fears were realized. One afternoon, I drove to pick up my son after school. I usually called him to make sure he was in the appropriate pick-up lane. This time was different. Instead of our usual chatter, he soberly informed me that his sister had been in an accident, and it was just around the corner from where I was. Cautiously, I turned the corner and saw ominous flashing red lights and yellow tape stretched across the road. I looked for a place to park and found a small vacant lot nearby. I sat in my car for a moment praying to Jesus: "Give me strength, dear Lord, to endure what I need to endure." Calmly, I walked out of the car and approached the scene. I needed to see if my daughter was okay. As I got out of the car, a police officer stopped me and told me, "The area is off limits." With unusual courage, I answered boldly, "I am her mother," and he let me through.

For some reason I felt an overwhelming sense of calm and control as I moved quickly toward the police and paramedics who were scrambling to get my daughter out of the mangled vehicle. As they began pulling her out on a stretcher, the crowd that gathered grew silent. In a state of calm numbness, I watched and waited. The blood streaming out of her ear did not eclipse the fact that her body lay eerily still. I waited, hushed and breathless. In that moment of silence, my daughter suddenly began screaming hysterically. To me, the sound was like a choir of angels singing! It was beautiful to me because it meant she was alive. I was elated. She was alive—that's all I cared about. Calmly, I followed the ambulance to the hospital, where doctors and nurses spent hours examining her. With the exception of the glass shards embedded in her face, my daughter was going to recover. In my hour of need, Jesus answered my prayer and gave me strength and courage to face the challenge before me. He protected my mind and heart from fear, keeping me calm in the midst of the storm.

> *"I can do all things through him who gives me strength"*
>
> **PHILIPPIANS 4:13 (NKJV)**

For many years this scripture remained fixed to my refrigerator as a reminder that with Him there is nothing I can't achieve or conquer. I have come to realize that God's achievements through me are greater than anything I could do alone. He alone is the Conqueror of fear, in life and in death. He is the Beacon of Hope in my despair.

> *"Be strong and courageous. Do not be*
> *afraid or terrified because of them, for*
> *the Lord your God goes with you; he will*
> *never leave you nor forsake you."*

DEUTERONOMY 31:6 (NIV)

In my hour of need, God delivered me. He lifted my fears and gave me hope and courage, he saw to it that I had the strength I needed to get through my daughter's accident. I am thankful and humbled as I know things could have turned out differently. I am thankful for the courage and commitment of the paramedics, police officers, and doctors who put themselves on the line to take care of my daughter. Their courage inspired me. God continues to inspire me.

LESSON 2

Faith

Growing up in a home full of chaos and abuse left me resentful and angry. I thirsted for something better but didn't know what it was. I needed safety, security, and consistency. I needed something other than what I was experiencing. That "something," once found, would ease my mind and soul with peace in a way I had never experienced. The world I lived in was void of compassion and callously collided with my interior divine self. Longing to be quenched with peace and tranquility, I needed a loving heart to nurture me but didn't know where to find it. I searched for a path that would lead me out of the darkness of my home life, and soon I found a group of young Christians who believed in a God greater than themselves. They demonstrated faith in a higher power who made sense of things that otherwise couldn't be explained. They seemed calm, assured, and whole, and I yearned for that feeling. I began attending their weekly meetings and realized my soul thirsted for what they had; values that reflected the goodness and love of God.

The quest for wholeness, however, proved challenging. This crooked path, I learned, was not a direct route to spiritual perfection, nor an endless stream of spiritual mountain top experiences. I failed often because it required trust and belief in something greater than myself, and trust, for me, was hard to come by. How could I trust a God who would allow me to be mocked, ridiculed, beaten, and molested? I wanted to believe that faith, once acquired, would flow seamlessly with patience, truth, humility, wisdom, and grace, but faith for me was difficult. The road back to my wholeness would zig-zag through the rocky terrain of my soul, where somedays I believed wholeheartedly and felt at peace, and other days I doubted God's power. Unsure of myself or a higher power, I yearned for the grace that faith promised, so I began asking God for signs when making important decisions.

I prayed endlessly when making the decision to leave my first marriage. I surrendered my will to God and prayed in faith for Him to give me answers. I told God I needed Him to be straight forward with me, not to "beat around the bush." He sent cardinals as a sign. For weeks, they slammed against my windows. I questioned whether this was the sign I had asked for? Were the cardinals telling me I was beating my head against the door? I wondered what it meant. As if being commanded by God, they showed up on the highway and at my brother's home. They followed me until I understood their message. Their color couldn't be ignored: red, like the saving blood of Jesus. In the fullness of faith, God delivered His message boldly as I had asked Him to. He wanted me to keep my faith, He let me know that no matter what happened, I would be okay because He would guide and protect me.

Faith, I learned, wills the invisible, visible. By asking for help, in fullness of faith, God reveals His divine plan and makes things known. The cardinals appeared after praying ceaselessly for help; they told me I was banging my head against the wall. I was trying to fix something that was not mine to fix. They signaled my need for faith in God, and when I understood their message, I began to feel certain that He would see me through that dark time. Whenever my faith wobbled the cardinals would show up in droves beckoning me to keep my mind and heart on God. After having experienced this "spirit-message," I began to trust, and I learned that faith requires humility, patience, and belief—humility to relinquish our will to His, patience to wait for His answers, and belief that the answers will come.

In order to bolster my faith, I needed to submit to God's divine orchestration, allowing events to unfold in His time, not mine. I learned that without faith in a higher power, we foolishly think we have control over our lives, and act according to our false, fear-based presumptions or misconceptions. Faith removes these obstacles by removing fear and replacing it with compassion for ourselves and others. When we live fully in faith, we live compassionately and can rest in Him, Who leads us away from the valley of dark shadows, into green pastures and still waters.

Like seeds, faith plants the essential belief that God will answer our prayers, not as we see fit, but as God wills for the good of His people. Since God is good, everything on earth works to His greater good. He sees no darkness as we see it—only hope, and love. "even the darkness is not dark to you; the night is bright as the day, for darkness is as light with you." *Psalm 139:12 (ESV)*

Living by faith helps us navigate the challenges of our emotions, relationships, financial woes, illnesses, and even death. Praying with faith helps keep our spiritual house free of anxieties, and delivers us from the evils of discontentment, self-absorption, and pride. Allowing God to guide us in our daily actions requires the faith that nothing is too big or too small for Him to handle. Faith casts hope into a dark world that often gets consumed by fear. Faith, the antidote to fear, eliminates darkness. When practiced daily, faith permeates our hearts, minds, and souls, and protects them from the anxiousness that accompanies our fears. My faith fades when I get stuck in my egotistical "I can do everything by myself" attitude, and this leaves me feeling lost and confused. Hope, in the absence of faith, provides a guiding light back to faith's door. Hope, like a lighthouse, helps us navigate life's dark waters, where otherwise we would end up moving in circles, often experiencing the same challenges over and over again. Like faith, hope is a necessary virtue for navigating turbulent waters. Without them both working in tandem, we fall victim to despair.

But even when practicing faith, setbacks are normal and humbling in their lessons, reminding us of our fallible human condition. This condition experienced by all believers teaches the necessary dependence on faith, even when it doesn't seem to be working. Faith becomes a friend, gently nudging us toward humility and seeing us through the best and worst times of our lives. Like a friend, I can call on faith whenever I need it, and even though I falter, God does not condemn me. He, like the father of the prodigal son, rejoices in my return, celebrating victory over darkness. Faith's power resides in the belief of a divine power, who loves us unconditionally and will take care of us spiritually and physically if we ask and believe. This act of trusting in something greater than our earthly selves becomes easier when we look back and see the work God has done in our lives. Like a dot-to-dot picture book, what once seemed like random unrelated events, start to form a clear picture, and we realize God had this picture in mind for us all along.

> *"Love bears all things, believes all things, hopes all things, endures all things."*
>
> **1 CO 13:7 (ESV)**

As I began to trust God and the picture He had in mind for my life, my faith grew, healthy friendships emerged, and my life flourished. The dark clouds of my childhood gave way to sunshine, and even though I still encounter many adversities, I have faith which I did not have before. Faith in a God who loves and accepts me for exactly who I am and promises life eternal in a kingdom where love wipes away the pain and sorrow of this earthly life.

Listening

"Close your eyes and hear My soul. I speak to you softly, and you do not hear. I whisper in your ear trying to reach you, but you do not hear. Close your eyes and speak to Me, and I will listen. I want to know you and hear your fears; I want you to know Me, but first you must listen. I speak through the trees, I speak through the animals, I speak through the windows of your soul, I send you messages, but you do not receive. Come to Me and listen, and I will tell you things so that you will understand. I want to hear you, and I want you to hear Me. That is my gift and when you have received it, pass it along...the gift of listening." (God)

God is all around us; He is everywhere, but some people do not see or hear Him. Although we have been blessed with eyes to see and ears to hear (Matthew 13:16), we choose not to quiet our minds in order to hear God's message to us. Many religions around the world practice listening by meditating so they may hear words of divine wisdom from their creator. When Mother Teresa was interviewed by Dan Rather, he asked her what she said to God when she prayed. She said, "Nothing, I just listen." He replied, "Then what does

God say to you?" "Nothing," she said, "He just listens." Her relationship with God mirrored a loving couple who give each other a listening ear even after many years of hearing the same stories. God wants that kind of relationship with us and waits patiently for us to confess our struggles and for us to listen to His answers.

In the presence of God, we are wrapped in a cocoon of love, being heard and understood without judgment. To pour out our hearts in an environment where we feel safe, and our feelings are not scrutinized under the harsh magnifying glass of another human, gives a feeling of worth and comfort. God wants us to pour out our hearts to Him and to listen for His wisdom. Essential to our souls awakening are our deepest feelings and fears, and if our hearts remain locked out of fear of judgment, we cannot discover our true selves through the light of God. In the silence of listening for answers, we may well be able to determine God's course for us and make better choices in our life. It's funny to note that *silent* and *listen* have the same letters, and in many ways are key to all healthy relationships. If we are not silent, we are not listening. Silence isn't just a matter of not speaking. For many, including myself, we have a parade of thoughts streaming through our minds while others are talking. Many times, if we are aware, we'll notice that instead of listening, we are actually waiting to talk. Like a garden filled with weeds, our thoughts can be invasive, scattered, and deeply troubling. God knows this and teaches us to meditate and listen to what He is saying. By keeping our minds quiet, doubts and fears are uprooted, and we discover a peace that resides beneath the chaos of our minds. We discover that when we are constantly talking, or waiting to talk, we are not listening. We discover when our thoughts are only directed toward ourselves, and not God, we are not listening.

Authentic listening proves difficult in our society because we live in a world of audio and visual stimulation. From the time we rise to the time we go to bed, we are bombarded with news reports, cell phone calls, social media, and a barrage of advertisements, all telling us how to think and feel. No wonder God wants us to be silent. He wants us to feel His presence through all of our senses. When we quiet our minds to experience what God is communicating, we begin to hear with spiritual ears and see with spiritual eyes.

> *"But blessed are your eyes, for they see: and your ears, for they hear. For verily I say unto you, that many prophets and righteous men have desire to see those things which ye see and have not seen them; and to hear those things which ye hear and have not heard them."*
>
> **MATTHEW 13 :16-17 (KJV)**

When our minds are silent, we leave room for God's message to enter in. Sometimes His message manifests in quiet ways, other times more boldly, but either way, if our minds are busy, we miss the message He is trying to convey. God's messages are not always verbal.

Sometimes an "aha" moment strikes us at the perfect time and leads us to an answer we longed for. Other times it may be a portent from a bird or an animal, like my visit from the cardinals. People don't always communicate verbally either. It has been documented that only seven percent of human communication is verbal, the rest is non-verbal. That is why we are told to hear and see with spiritual eyes. If we quiet our minds and our souls, we can be present to all the spiritual languages God speaks. Because the mind and the soul work together to effectively hear and decipher God's word. "…Be still and know that I am God;…" Psalm 46:10 (NIV) Sometimes, stillness awakens us to His presence, and we become aware of what He is trying to tell us.

Even though we each may ask for similar things, God doesn't always give everyone the same answer in the same way. If you can imagine that everyone needs different lessons to grow in their spirituality, then it makes sense that our understanding of God's Word, may speak to our individual situations. Sometimes He gives us what we need to hear in the moment we need to hear it. Other times we may get and understanding from a friend or co-worker. Either way, God is not looking for conformity of thought with everyone; He knows we have different ways of experiencing His Word. He wants each of us to listen with our hearts and bring to the table our individual understanding of His love as we've experienced it. Our gift to the world is sharing that love by sharing what we hear God beckoning us to do.

Our unique understanding of the Word shared with others adds variety to God's spiritual garden, because a garden cannot survive with only one type of plant, for if disease strikes, all the plants perish. So it is, with our spiritual perspectives. Each perspective of spiritual truth, when combined with others, strengthens our faith as we learn and grow from it. When we listen with our hearts and unite our different perspectives, we join together in harmony to face the adversities of this earthly life. God wants each of us to hear His Word, but only as it applies to us. For example, when a mother is struggling with her children and prays to God, she may hear Him saying her child needs more discipline. Yet another mother may pray the exact same prayer and hear God telling her the child needs more love. Any of us who have raised more than one child can testify that each child, though unique, needs both discipline and love to grow.

As we hear and pay attention to God's personal message, God will introduce us to others who can help on our journey. Part of the mystery and wonder of God's love is Him leading us to other Christian followers, for who better to lead a man out of suffering than another man who has suffered in the same way? This is exemplified through the life and death of Jesus who suffered because He brought God's message to God's people in a new way. He listened to God and knew what we needed to hear; that God is a loving Father instead of a wrathful one.

The Living Word of God lives on in each generation

and takes on new meaning as we listen and hear what God is telling us in that particular time or place. Opening our spiritual senses to the mystical and practical messages God has to offer us means listening with our hearts, minds, and souls and finding silence and solace in a noisy world. If we understand the wisdom that "There is a time to be silent and a time to speak," Ecclesiastes 3:7 (NIV) we may, if we're aware, hear God's wonderful message calling us to "...Be still and know that I am God..." Psalms 46-10 (NIV) If we learn to listen, we may be anointed with divine wisdom to help us navigate the fallen world in which we live.

CHAPTER 8

"A Time to Weep"

Have courage for the great sorrows of life
and patience for the small ones;
And when you have laboriously accomplished
your daily task,
Go to sleep in peace. God is awake.

VICTOR HUGO

LESSON 1

Pain & Suffering

I don't know why but listening to a soulful operatic aria or a lone cello compels me to weep. This type of music magically conveys passion and heartache and instantly transports me to a place in my heart where a world of pain and suffering reside. The minor chords speak of something mystically beautiful beyond words, and I cannot imagine a world without the creative artistry which embodies and reflects the suffering of human life. For somewhere in the midst of the pain lies the beauty of compassion, truth, and love.

In my life I've endured physical and emotional abuse, as well as abandonment. Like most, I suffered long after the offenses occurred and believed God should not have allowed the events to happen, for they were too cruel and painful. Pridefully, I suffered as I believed no one else had. However, when I believed no one cared about me or my life, God entered in, like the sun breaking through dark clouds. He brought peace and tranquility to the anguished garden of my soul. In the hour of my need, I experienced the magnitude of God's love, as God appeared like a mirror to my humanity. He showed me He had chosen suffering too because He loved me. As this revelation came to me, I wept, and tears fell like rain upon the desert of my soul. In each desperate hour of suffering, God showed me compassion, love, hope, and joy. Now, although I don't look forward to suffering, I have begun to understand the meaning of suffering in my life. I understand that it builds maturity, endurance, faith, and character.

> *"Not only that, but we rejoice in our sufferings, knowing that suffering produces endurance, and endurance produces character, and character produces hope, and hope does not put us to shame, because God's love has been poured into our hearts through the Holy Spirit who has been given to us."*

ROMANS 5:3-5 (ESV)

Suffering is usually not a one-time event; most of us will endure many types of suffering in our lives. In my life, I have suffered pain, abuse, betrayal, death, illness, indifference, neglect and abandonment. But no matter how many times I suffered, every time I connected to the Divine through prayer, I found compassion. God enabled me to find hope instead of despair, love instead of hate, and forgiveness instead of revenge. Amidst the human darkness, with discord all around me, I heard the voice of God cry out the same way a cello's mournful voice cries out when the bow caresses its strings. Touched by God's hand, I felt His warmth and kindness surrounding me in the harsh wilderness of the world in which I grew up.

The selfishness and sin of the people I grew up with led to my suffering. And the selfishness and sin of others led to the suffering of Christ. In life, the suffering we endure paradoxically teaches us about love because the way we treat others manifests either in love or suffering. The more we mistreat others, knowingly or unknowingly, because of our self-centeredness, the more we create suffering. Each time I sin, I cause suffering. Whether the sin is known or unknown, or whether it is a thought or a deed. When we sin against another human, we are sinning against God, and that creates suffering.

> *"...Truly I tell you whatever you did for one of the least of these brothers and sisters of mine, you did for me."*
> **MATTHEW 25:40 (NIV)**

God loves us in spite of ourselves and was willing to send His son to suffer on the cross as a testimony to the love He has for us. Who among us would lay our sinless child on the altar of pain and agony to atone for our sins? Yet God in his infinite love did just that. Our suffering teaches us a beautiful lesson in empathy, and empathy leads us to the Garden of Compassion, for God, ourselves, and others.

To those who have suffered illness, death, destruction, shame, despair, loneliness, pain, addiction, hatred, terror, or trauma, know that God is with you and in you. You are worthy of His love and compassion.

I could not tell you this if I had not suffered. For this reason, I thank Him for my suffering and find peace and joy in that.

Andrew Lloyd Webber's Requiem mass "Pie Jesus," which premiered in 1985 was written in memory of the composer's father who died in 1982. It remains one of my favorite pieces of sacred music. When I first heard this requiem, I felt my heart expanding to something rich and beautiful, for I felt its power, compassion, and pain and sensed the love of Christ in it. In the beginning of the piece, I imagined Christ struggling as he carried the cross, then later, when the music begins to swell, I sensed the risen Christ transcending the world of suffering and entering into the eternal Garden where hope, love, and peace reside.

In pain and suffering Christ lights the path to our darkness and manifests hope like a glowing candle in a dark room which disperses the shadows and sustains us. Without the candle of hope, pain and suffering can lead to depression and keep us trapped in darkness. Just a tiny flicker of hope, like the candle, can lift our spirits, bringing wholeness and happiness back into our lives. In her book *Emotional Freedom*, Judith Orloff says hope is like opening your arms to a bouquet of flowers; everything smells better, tastes better, and you are physically lighter and perkier. She talks about the contagion of hope, as opposed to the contagion of depression, and how you can catch their respective energies without even knowing it.

Physical, emotional, and spiritual pain will always

be an intrinsic part of our existence, yet by choosing faith over doubt and hope over hopelessness, we can sustain the inevitable pain and suffering in life and spread the mystical energy that God has cultivated in us. We can learn that suffering and pain are simply a means to an end, to strengthen our spiritual constitution, so we can empower and encourage others when they suffer. Our suffering is not in vain any more than Jesus' suffering was in vain. How we conquer it is a testimony to God's grace. We rise above our suffering, not by ignoring it, but by transforming it into something beautiful, like a piece of music sung with the depth of soul of its creator.

CHAPTER 9

"A Time to Laugh"

*The most wasted days
is one without laughter*

EE CUMMINGS

LESSON 1

Rejoice

Of all the things I am grateful for, laughter and joy are two blessings which I could not live without. As the crown jewels in God's divine kingdom, laughter and joy remind us in the midst of chaos, there is something to celebrate. These divine heaven-grown remedies feed our souls and sustain our spirits. If we can learn to laugh and find joy amongst all the madness that surrounds us, we have won the great battle against darkness. One of the verses in the Bible, "Rejoice in the Lord always; and again, I say, Rejoice!" Philippians 4:4 (KJV) reminds us that God takes pleasure in our pleasure.

Out of curiosity, I decided to look up the definition of *rejoice* which read: "to feel or show great joy or delight." Following the definition was a list of synonyms: *happiness, pleasure, joy, gladness, delight, elation, cheer, jubilation, euphoria, delirium, ecstasy, rapture, exuberance, exultation, glory, triumph, celebration, revelry, merrymaking, and festivity.* Astounded by this list, I wondered if this is what Paul meant when he said to rejoice always? If this is the case, I have a lot of work to do because I struggle with rejoicing always. Negative thoughts fight for control of my mind, and sometimes it's hard to keep them out. Even as I write this, I see the irony of rejoicing being hard work for me. I have the tendency to take things too seriously, including myself, yet I know science has proven the chemicals produced in tears of laughter are much different than the chemicals produced in the tears of sorrow. Laughter and joy release feel good endorphins that aid in reducing pain and other ailments. Depression, on the other hand, can cause pain and reduce our lust for life. Rejoicing is good for our health. What more do we need to convince us of the command to rejoice?

Some of the biggest events in our lives are filled with joy and we rejoice: the birth of a child, a marriage, or graduation. Other things we remember with joy are events such as winning a championship football or basketball game, landing our first big job, or even celebrating our first kiss. But what of everyday life? How do we, as Paul suggests, "rejoice always?" In Ann Voscamp's book, *A Thousand Gifts*, she recounts a difficult time in her life when she could not find joy. Her journey led her to finding everyday gifts that were hidden as God's treasures amid the struggle of raising five children on a working-farm in Canada. She discovered all she had to do was look for joy amongst the chaos of her daily life. She was so moved by this discovery, she decided to make a list of a thousand gifts as a reminder of God's presence in her life.

When gardening I often come across joyful surprises buried beneath the soil: an old rusted hoe left during a rainstorm last year, a metal roller skate (the kind I had as a kid), or a piece of old pottery shard from the 1950s. Each time I come across these treasures, I stop and reflect on the history of these hidden jewels. It always brings me great joy to find such things I have forgotten. As a reminder of the simple joys in everyday living, I have displayed these treasures in various places around my house.

These treasures remind me of the joys and gifts God has hidden in our daily lives. Most of these things we take for granted because we don't pay attention, or we focus on the negative instead. As I unearthed my garden journal that lay buried for so many years, I discovered another gift. I had written my own list of joys of God's presence in my everyday life. After reading Ann's book, I realize I need to keep this list alive. Here is the list I discovered…with a few additions.

1. The smell of fresh baking bread
2. The feel of freshly washed sheets
3. The sight of a robin in snow announcing the coming of Spring
4. A warm fire in wintertime
5. A hot bowl of chili on a cold rainy day
6. The scent of roses outside my front door
7. Watching a young mother cart four children into a grocery store, and being thankful I am past that stage
8. My cat jumping in my lap every time I sit down
9. Identifying the seedlings in my garden

10. The joy of quiet time to reflect, write, and meditate
11. Dancing and singing to God's music
12. Roasting marshmallows and making s'mores
13. Getting my family to church on time each Sunday
14. Seeing the look on my grandson's face when he shouts "Gam-gam!"

As a spiritual practice, reflecting on everyday gifts helps to fill our souls. When we feel thirsty for the love of Christ, we can drink from His well of laughter and joy. It is amazing when I shift my focus and rejoice in God's gifts, how my overall demeanor changes.

> *"This is the day the LORD has made; let us be glad and rejoice in it!"*
> **PSALM 118:24 (ESV)**

Drink Up!

Drink up! Let the multitudes of life's treasures fill your soul. Drink up! Breathe in the Holy Spirit until you have felt the presence of the Lord. Drink up! Feel the love of the world surround you; consume the beauty of the day. Drink up! Be open to all miracles great and small. Drink up! Dance to the rhythm of life, the beat of your heart. Drink up! Know that the Lord our God is with you always, constant and willing to serve. Drink up!

The Lord is a never-ending well of spiritual sustenance, and by keeping our hearts and minds open, we become vessels to receive the Living Waters of His love. Everything good in this world is a gift from God, and God's gifts, immeasurable in scope and time, fill our lives with meaning and purpose.

As human's thirst for something beyond what the material world can provide, they fail to realize that the tangibles they believed would make them happy leave them hollow. They discover that time spent trying to fill a spiritual void with material goods becomes fruitless, a temporary fix that eventually leaves a bigger void. Yet like addicts, their thirst is never quenched because they are looking to the wrong things to fill them up. They fail to realize that when we don't leave room for God's love that surrounds us every day, our souls die of thirst, because what we are really longing for is something that brings meaning to our existence. Our souls beg us to drink up God's abundant love, but we, in our plight to find happiness elsewhere, ignore it.

> *"I can do all things through him who strengthens me."*
>
> PHIL-4:13 (ESV)

When we drink the Living Waters which sustains our spiritual life, we are nurtured and strengthened through both the valleys and the mountain tops of our lives. God's never-ending supply of love, wisdom, and forgiveness fills the crevices in our broken hearts and comforts us when we are alone. By quenching the thirst in our hearts with God's love, nothing is impossible. He gives us strength and courage to endure the hardships and take risks we otherwise may not have taken. When we allow God's spirit to flow through us, we can watch with excitement how that love overflows and spills onto other souls who need quenching. When we choose to drink up the Living Waters, we are choosing life over death, positive over negative, enthusiasm over boredom, and sustenance over complaint. When we allow God's life to flow through us, we can watch with excitement as His spirit takes us to new heights we never dreamed of before.

When we drink the Living Waters of God's spirit and truth, the eyes of our hearts are opened, and things we never understood before, become clear. We come to see and understand that humans are connected just like all waters of the world, that flow into the oceans. When we drink up God's spirit, the earth and all that is in it, becomes ours as long as our hearts stay true to the truth of our Redeemer. By drinking up the true spirit of God we discover the true meaning of life and revel in its possibilities. No longer are we afraid, for God is with us and will see us through turbulent times. Without God to sustain us, we suffer needlessly. When we drink up the Holy Spirit and flow with the Living Water of God's unending love, we drink up all that God so pleasurably gives us. It is ours for the taking, the free gift of unending love. Drink up!

CHAPTER 10

"A Time to Seek"

For in the true nature of things,
if we will rightly consider,
every green tree is far more glorious,
than if it were made of gold and silver.

MARTIN LUTHER

LESSON 1

Spiritual Truth

The spiritual and divine truth of God is Love. When lived, sought, and embraced, it binds us together as humans. When we yield to its power, we fulfill our destiny. When we separate from it, we separate from ourselves, God, and others. Living in spiritual truth is accepting things as they are in an imperfect world; it is also accepting that God's ways are not our ways and can never be fully comprehended. When we are reborn in the Spirit of truth, we aren't just born once, but again and again, as each new grain of truth reveals an infinite other. As we are reborn, we fill the world with love in the same way raindrops join together to satiate the dry earth.

Living in truth requires opening our hearts, yielding to our inner guidance system, and attuning ourselves to God's voice yearning to be heard. Our submission to our divine inner voice becomes a submission to God's will rather than our own. When aroused by divine truth, our inner world becomes a symphony of harmonic chords which stir our hearts to follow the direction of the Divine Conductor's hand. The song of humanity, being love, reveals the tenderness of the human heart and the benevolence of our Creator, Who seeks our soul's salvation through His son, Jesus Christ.

> *"God grant me the Serenity to accept the things I cannot change, the courage to change the things I can, and the Wisdom to know the difference."*

REINHOLD NIEBUHR

Seeking truth in everything, through the eyes of God, embraces the imperfect world in which we live by manifesting an attitude of acceptance, rather than judgement. In a world full of contradictions and confusion, prayers like the "Serenity Prayer" teach us the true meaning of acceptance, courage, and wisdom. This prayer, spread through sermons and churches in the 1930s and 40s, was later used in Alcoholics Anonymous and other twelve-step programs. The prayer tells us we are not in control and must relinquish ourselves to a higher power of truth if we are to find peace within ourselves. The search for spiritual truth is accepting fully who we are in our weakness and faulty perspectives. It can be painful and difficult to examine ourselves in the light of pure love, yet if we are willing to accept and love ourselves exactly as we are, then we can accept the same in others as well. The quest for authenticity helps us discover the treasures of our own buried courage and wisdom as we open up to God and others without falsification.

> *"For my thoughts are not your thoughts,*
> *neither are your ways My ways, declares*
> *the Lord. For as the heavens are higher*
> *than the earth, So are My ways higher*
> *than your ways, And My thoughts than*
> *your thoughts."*

ISAIAH 55:8-9 (ESV)

The spiritual truth of scripture tells us that whatever we think, see, or do, is not always in sync with the truth of God, for our thoughts and ways are not His. In order to align ourselves with God's truth, we must open up to His ways, His thoughts, and His divine mystery. This mystery intersects with our lives and reveals a glimpse of God's presence in our world. Even when aligned with holy truth, our understanding, through the lens of our humanness, is limited to the confines of our earthly state of being. The infinite truth, power, and love of God is vastly underestimated. He reaches beyond time and space in dimension and scope such that we humans could never comprehend. When we think we have found divine truth, and understand it, we have only sifted one grain of sand on an endless seashore.

Truth then, becomes a never-ending quest, a reality not of an earthly dimension, but divine. In eternal time, I believe divine truth will be known to those who have kept the faith. In the meantime, decoding divine truth takes patience and practice. As long as we keep our gaze on God's perspective, we may if we're lucky get a glimpse of Heaven on earth. But only in the state of Heaven's truth will the meaning and purpose of our lives become clear. What we may think of as meaningless, may be, in spiritual truth, monumental. One can imagine this truth by imagining a singular drop of rain. It alone may not satiate the earth, but thousands will. Falling together, yet separate, each drop has a destiny to fulfill. The path they follow is without question a divine one. Happily, and obediently, like children, each drop trusts and follows the instruction of its Creator. We, like raindrops, are small, but many. When guided by spiritual truth, we may bind together and satiate the earth with God's love.

LESSON 2

Comfort

After spending the morning in the hot summer sun pulling weeds, pruning, and replanting, I take refuge for a moment in the comfort of my home. I pour myself a glass of water, snack on some fruit, and renew my energy. Afterward, I head outside to resume my gardening. Later in the day, I shower, do a little housekeeping, and take a break to enjoy a cup of tea and catch up on my reading. Although I am not rich by any stretch, I have a comfortable life and appreciate the opportunity to provide a haven for my family. I am grateful that I live in comfort, but I remember a time when things weren't so comfortable.

When I started my business, I had a lot of gumption and little money. With two babies in tow, I traveled across the country and sold antiques at various flea markets. I drove an old utility van, which I converted into a sleeper for longer journeys. Some days, I drove twelve to sixteen hours to reach my destination. While on the road, I nursed, changed diapers and provided entertainment for my children by pointing to cows, horses, barns, and anything of interest I was lucky enough to spot. Each time I left for a market, I emptied my home of all its furniture. If the show was successful, I returned to an empty house; if it was not, I had furniture to sit on. In an unpredictable market, my future was clouded with uncertainty and worry because I wasn't sure from month to month if I could pay my bills. I suffered anxiety and worry over providing a comfortable home for my family. The house we lived in was old, cold, and drafty. To keep warm during the winter, we slept on a make-shift pallet in front of a wood burning stove, one of the few sources of heat in our house.

During these uncertain times, I prayed heavily for God to provide for us. Never knowing the outcome of my prayers, I counted on my faith to keep me going. Looking back, I can easily see God's hand in my life. He heard my prayers and answered them. When my bank account was down to the last penny and I hadn't a clue as to how I would survive, suddenly out of nowhere a buyer would show up spending just enough money to get me through the month. We never went hungry, although we ate a lot of macaroni and cheese, and we always had a roof over our heads. I came to understand that through life's patterns of ups and downs, God is by our side. He watches over us and protects us whether we are aware of it or not.

Eventually, I made enough money to invest a small amount in savings. I enjoyed more free time, and during this time God led me to a local church. There I deepened my faith and understood more fully the boundless blessings I had received in my life. I trusted that no matter the circumstances, God would provide for me and my family. Each step I took on this faith journey provided me with comfort and peace of mind. The church where God led me to, was a comfortable fit and provided a safe place to deepen my spiritual awareness. Eventually I felt compelled to find a way to help others in the way God had helped me. I learned that there will always be others in need who yearn for the love of God. Many children go to bed hungry or without proper nutrition. Many will not have a home or adequate clothing in winter to keep warm. Some people work two and three jobs just to make ends meet, and many of our elderly must choose between paying their bills or buying medicine. For them, life is not so comfortable.

I began to understand how vital community worship was to me. I learned that faith in God, and sharing that faith with others through the body of Christ, builds a faith family that comforts us in times of need. For people in need, a church can be a welcoming port in a storm and provide necessary provisions when they are going through difficult times. During the aftermath of hurricane Katrina, many local churches, including the church I attended, fed, sheltered, and ministered to those who had escaped the floods with nothing but the clothes on their backs. Not only had they lost everything, but they had been separated from their loved ones as well. Members of the church became like a second family to these refugees, and through our love and support, helped those in need with prayer and offerings. This is just one example of how God provides comfort through the body of Christ's church. The church also provides comfort to those with illnesses or dying loved ones and provides spiritual education to those in need of God's Word. Psalm 46:1-3 states: "God is our refuge and strength, a very present help in trouble." (NKJV) We further read in Isaiah 41:10, "So do not fear, for I am with you; do not be dismayed, for I am your God. I will strengthen you and help you; I will uphold you with my righteous right hand." (NIV)

Without guidance from the church and its leaders, I wouldn't have studied the Bible. I wouldn't be able to rely on God's words for comfort and love during difficult times. When we come to church, it is as if Christ is comforting us in His arms as a mother's arms provide comfort, warmth, and safety for her children. We come to church to be strengthened and renewed into Christ's body so that we may strengthen and comfort others.

Even though I am past the years of financial worry, I still need comforting. I still need to hear God's words that strengthen and support me when I am weary, lonesome, or struggling with difficult issues. I have since moved to a different town, but I found a new church that welcomes me and provides solace when I need it. From time to time I work in my garden and still think about my little drafty house that provided shelter for my family for so many years. Now when I am down, I recite my favorite scripture over and over, as it brings me great comfort.

*"The Lord is my shepherd; I shall
not want.
He maketh me to lie down in green
pastures: he leadeth me beside the
still waters.
He restoreth my soul: he leadeth me
in the paths of righteousness for his
name's sake.
Yea though I walk through the valley of
the shadow of death, I will fear no evil,
for Thou art with me; thy rod and thy
staff they comfort me.
Thou preparest a table before me in the
presence of mine enemies: thou anointest
my head with oil; my cup runneth over.
Surely goodness and mercy shall follow
me all the days of my life: and I will
dwell in the house of the Lord forever."*

PSALM 23 (KJV)

LESSON 3

Treasure

"Ask and it will be given you; seek and you will find; knock, and it will be opened to you: for everyone who asks receives; and he who seeks finds...."

MATTHEW 7:7-8 (NKJV)

When I became a Christian at fifteen, I was very happy to hear that God was willing to give me anything I asked for. *Wow*, I thought, *a new prom dress, a passing grade in my algebra class, and a date with the cute guy in my English class. What a deal!* All that was asked of me was to believe in Christ; sounds simple, right? But as I grew in faith, developing a Godly conscience was trickier than I thought. A little thing called guilt cropped up whenever I took more than I gave. I noticed no matter how much I received from God, I always wanted more. I didn't like knowing this about myself, so I began to research this "greed" phenomenon. I discovered I was not the only one with this problem. In our modern culture, the material or "treasure- trap" is real. Americans have a "possession obsession" as illustrated in Randy Alcorn's, *The Treasure Principle*. He

115

cited that the average American shops six hours a week while spending a mere forty minutes playing with their children. By age twenty, we've seen over one million advertisements, and more Americans have declared bankruptcy than graduated from college.

Jesus says: "Lay not up for yourselves treasures on earth, where moth and rust doth corrupt, and where thieves break through and steal; but lay up for yourselves treasures in heaven, where neither moth nor rust doth corrupt, and where thieves do not break through nor steal." Matthew 6:19-20 (KJV) In the wake of today's volatile weather patterns, no one knows better than those whose homes have been destroyed, that material possessions are fleeting. Most learn quickly that what really matters is not the love of money or stuff, but the love for our family, friends, neighbors and pets. Because God's treasures are everlasting, we know that nothing can destroy them. When we invest our time, talent, and treasure in the Divine Kingdom, our souls rejoice each time we give to charity or help someone in need. Rather than allowing the trappings of earthly treasures to control us, we are called to trust in God, who teaches us that loving others has much more worth than owning things that rot and rust.

Wealth and all its frills are a blessing from God but can easily become a form of false worship when we elevate our riches to the status of idols. When we bend our knee to wealth rather than God, our blessing may turn into darkness. There are over one hundred Bible verses that warn about the relationship between idolatry and money, yet I am perplexed that there are churches that preach a "Prosperity Gospel" where congregants are told that financial blessing is the will of God, and financial donations will increase one's material wealth. This sad theology I believe misleads people into thinking that money is all that matters. For sure, money is a blessing, but the blessing can be used to help people, rather than purchasing multiple homes filled with more stuff. What we do with, and how we invest our blessings is spiritually important. In Matthew 25:14-30, Jesus tells the parable of three slaves whose master gives them talents (money) while he is away. Each man received talents of differing amounts. The first two slaves were industrious and doubled their money, but the last slave hid his talents in the earth because he was afraid. When the master returned, he questioned the slaves to see how well they managed their money. He was very pleased with the first two, while gravely disappointed with the last. The parable is about how we trust God with the blessings He has bestowed on us.

This lesson is near and dear to my heart as it reminds me of the first summer of my antiques business at a flea market in New England, I sold $25,000 worth of goods in three days. Feeling rich, I spent the summer playing golf, eating out, and shopping. I purchased luxury items I normally wouldn't have bought, and by the end of summer, I had squandered away my hard-earned money. By October, my account had dwindled to zero, and I drove to Chicago desperately trying to sell a 1950s sofa set. I sold the set for $700, which was just enough to pay bills. My prayers during that time were fervent and full of repentance for how foolish I'd been, and I promised God I would do better, if given another chance. I have to admit, having the freedom to spend money on whatever whim caught my eye was fun, but I also experienced how addicting money could be. It wasn't as if I bought one nice thing and stopped. The more I bought, the more I wanted. It was a bottomless pit of greed and selfishness. I am glad now that I had that experience, for it taught me lessons I needed to learn about money and its trappings.

> *"Instruct those who are rich in this present world not to be conceited or to fix their hope on the uncertainty of riches, but on God who richly supplies us with all things to enjoy."*
>
> **1 TIMOTHY 6:17 (NASB)**

The supply we receive from God is a magnitude of wealth that cannot be measured in earthly terms. Money or goods purchased, will never bring joy, spiritual comfort, love, grace, or forgiveness. Their temporal nature, short term and shallow, serves as a warning to us to fix our eyes on Heaven where our true treasure lies.

CHAPTER 11

"A Time to Keep"

*I am certain of nothing
But the holiness of the
Hearts affections and
The truth of
Imagination-what the
Imagination seizes as
Beauty must be truth-
Whether it exists
Before or not.*

JOHN KEATS

LESSON 1

Imagine

As children of God, we are born with divine creativity and imagination. When cultivated, our hope-filled imagination has the ability to change the world in profound ways. Our imaginative dreams help keep the bud of hope alive in a world filled with despair. Just below the surface of our muddy cynicism and doubt, imagination, hope, and creativity sustain the life-giving blood of divine potential. Without divine imagination and creativity, we are left to wander in a desert of dry bones. We feel depleted and worn out, never really knowing why. Our sense of purpose is lost because our imagination has been buried. Yet when we think of God, we think of the Supreme Creator, who imagined everything that came into being. He imagined the heavens, the earth, the oceans, and the animals. He imagined a garden with a man and a woman made in His image.

Each time I gaze at a magnificent sunset, stunning mountain view, or birth of a child, I am called to witness the miracle of God's imagination. Made in His image, we carry that imagination in us. We, like God, are imaginative creative beings. When we are at our best, we are creating, whether a delicious meal, painting, or novel. Creativity and imagination feed our souls, and when our souls are fed, we shine our brightest.

Creativity and imagination also keep dreams of divine ideals alive, allowing us to achieve things we never thought possible. Divine imagination beckons the world to bloom into a place where children do not go hungry, violence does not exist, and all peoples of all nations live in harmony. When we partake in the divine imagination of caring for each other in a fallen world, we, like God, bless all people and all nations. (Deuteronomy. 28-10) Knowing God loves and blesses all of us, we can, imagine a world where we bless each other with loving kindness rather than hateful judgement.

As adults we tend to lose our vivid childlike imagination; we see the world as concrete and unchangeable. Our creative vision becomes muddied by mistrust, allowing fear to hinder hope, and creativity, as dark cynicism, corrupts our hopeful imagination. Mercilessly, fear attacks our optimism, and we wallow in depression or defeat. In order to counter this attack, we are called to create the world God intended by finding our way back to hope, imagination, and creativity. We are called to use our imaginations to adapt to or change reality, rather than reality conquering divine imagination.

As a child, I had an active imagination. I spent hours on my swing, soaring above the treetops. I felt connected to the sky, clouds, and warm sun. My world came alive with wonder as I imagined myself a mother, an adventurer, a dancer, and an actress. These adolescent dreams captivated my mind, and I play-acted them out in my innocent, make-believe world. I pretended nothing was impossible, so I believed all things possible!

God makes it very clear that we are to become like children if we are to enter the Kingdom. (Matthew 18:3) In so doing, we must learn to use our imaginations. We must visualize what could exist without the knowledge as to how to create it. I don't suppose the Wright brothers had any idea how or when their aircraft was going to fly, yet they imagined a flying machine and believed they could make it happen. They envisioned a future where humans could fly across continents, reaching distant shores in record time. Never in their hard work or trial and error did they have a guarantee as to the outcome, yet they never gave up faith in their dream.

Our dreams and imagination can be light-filled promises for the future. When we appeal to the higher elevation of our minds and hearts, we enlighten our imagination, and by doing so, embrace all that is good. When we open our eyes to life as hopeful and full of possibilities, our dreams radiate promises of a brighter tomorrow. With higher ideals of divine thought, we have the ability to change ourselves, relationships, and the world. If we dream and imagine it, it will happen. If we believe and trust in a loving God Who will help guide and protect us, it will happen. If it is good, it is from God, as God cannot imagine nor partake in anything that is not for the greater good.

The world is full of negative energy that saps life out of the hopeful imagination. Using our creativity to change the world helps defeat the enemy of our souls by changing the negativity that surrounds us into something positive. We can imagine loving our neighbors even though they annoy us, or our children even though they misbehave. We can imagine piercing through judgement, condemnation, and shame by forgiving ourselves and others for past and present mistakes. While manifesting love in our imagination, we invite the light of the Holy Spirit, and in this light, God begins to mold and transform us as we imagine ourselves stepping out of darkness and into light. With a hopeful imagination, we are glorified because God our Creator is glorified.

Dr. Martin Luther King Jr., a freedom fighter for equality, had such an imagination. He had a divine dream that men and women of all colors, creeds, religious backgrounds, and cultures, would hold hands and unite in the common cause of liberty and justice for all. He maintained his divine vision that all people are created equal and should be given equal access to the pursuit of happiness. Out of love for God and his people and hate for the dark injustices of racism, Dr. King gave his life for the hopeful ideas of his imagination. What remained in his wake was an undaunted enthusiasm that secured hope and equality for generations to come. His fight, though not over, lives on in the hopeful imagination. Similar to King's dream, John Lennon's song "Imagine" portrays a world of peace, with nothing to kill or die for. He imagines a brotherhood of man seeking to eliminate hunger and greed, and he imagines a world in which we share the earth's resources. He claims he is a dreamer, but declares he is not the only one.

We ascend to the divine heights of our imagination when we dream the impossible dream. Combined with hope and creativity, that dream becomes a reality when blessed by God. When our creative imagination is cultivated with love, we strengthen our hearts to bear all things, hope in all things, believe in all things, and endure all things (1 Corinthian) in order to make the world a better place. God's hopeful imagination created the world, and we, as creative beings made in His image, are called to unearth our God-given imagination and maintain it with love.

LESSON 2

The Gift of Time

God tells us, regardless of exterior circumstances, we are to live in the present moment, a sacred space of awareness allowing us to be, in the here and now. However, many of us spend our days worrying about the future or ruminating over the past and sadly miss the opportunity to live in the moment in which we are fully alive. We don't imagine at any time our lives may drastically change, yet suddenly we may find ourselves in circumstances facing a serious disease or suffering profound loss. Whatever the case, precisely in these moments we are afforded the opportunity to learn the truth about the present.

Often, due to unforeseen circumstances, we learn the futility of our worries which may never materialize, or the waste of time ruminating over a past we cannot change. Living in the now, especially during times of great challenge, helps us gain perspective of the gift of the present moment, as we learn to deal with our situation, one day, one hour, or one minute at a time. Living in the sacred now mercifully allows us space to feel the magnitude of our emotions, where otherwise we may attempt to contain in order to control them. In the face of uncertainty, as we tend to our emotions, the present allows us space to depend on God, friends, and family to help us through. Only when we appreciate the divine meaning of the present in which God resides, can we appreciate fully our fragile existence and how precious every breath is.

Imagine if we could learn to live this way every day. Imagine with every breath we take, embracing a more calm, centered way of living that creates a space for God to reside in our awareness. Imagine giving up our anxieties and trusting our Creator every minute of every day to take care of us. In His loving mercy, God instructs us not to be anxious about tomorrow, for tomorrow will be anxious for itself. "...Sufficient for the day is its own trouble." Matthew 6:34 (ESV)

Each day, as the clock ticks, past yields to present, and present yields to future. Even as I write, I realize each word laid carefully down instantly becomes the past, and unlike our lives which cannot be re-written nor foretold, I can choose to spend the present moment re-writing or imagining what comes next. But if I don't write in this moment, which is the only moment I have, my story will never be told.

Yielding to the present requires patience and focus on the things in life that are spiritually important. In each moment we can learn to separate the dross from the gold and glean the sacred lesson God is teaching us. Knowing God's Word, the bread of life, helps us decipher and discern what is important in the eyes of God. When studied daily, the Word awakens us to its mystical power, and opens the eyes of our heart, enabling us to love fully in the moment in which we are alive.

Being aware of God in the present is a gift which gives us a glimpse into the Divine, where infinite love infuses everything. All our senses fully awakened reveal His love, as well as a mystical understanding that manifests a spiritual "knowing," which can only be realized in the present moment in which we live. God's gift of the present nourishes and sustains us through our daily toil and trials, as we are blessed to see His divine gift for what it really is. In the same way we cannot eat our meals in advance, nor change the meal we ate yesterday, our spiritual sustenance becomes the feast of the now.

When living in God's now, the invisible becomes visible and His profound presence illuminates all that is and will ever be. When we fix our gaze on the light of truth and love, in the here and now, we become like children in the garden of His divine creation. Each and every moment, filled with awe and wide-eyed wonder, becomes a discovery of the abundance of God's love. Nothing in the mystical now goes unnoticed, as God's magnificent creation reveals God's glory and imagination. Spellbound by miraculous sunsets, meadows laced with wildflowers, or water cascading down chiseled rock, all creation unveils its glory in the moment of our present awareness.

If you've ever watched children play, they seem to know this instinctively. While we push them into our neurotic world of rumination and worry over past and future, they explore with undaunted enthusiasm the present world in which they live. Incapable of guilt or worry, children see their world as a magical playground, full of awe and wonder. They celebrate each moment with curiosity, marveling at the beauty of butterflies' wings, the taste of the earth, or the rough bark of a tree. Their fidelity to the present is a lesson for us all because God tells us to become like children before we enter the kingdom (Matt. 18:3).

Imagine choosing to live each day as an opportunity to connect with the divine in every present moment we are alive. By living in the present, we can be clothed in the Spirit, feast with the angels, and savor the gift of time that God has so lovingly provided for us. This gift can be invested wisely by spending it with care and attention to the people, places, and things that surround us.

Exciting new discoveries can be made when we honor each precious moment, knowing it will never return. Every day as I walk outside, my soul swells at new discoveries in my garden. I feel giddy when observing a young seedling emerging from its earthly cocoon or spy the clues of tattered leaves left by a hungry grasshopper. Keeping my mind focused and alert, I never sense a dull moment in the life of my garden. When I am not digging plants or pulling weeds, I'm content in observing the landscape and making notes for future ideas.

Each day brings new and wonderous events and if I

am not present, I miss them. Last Spring, while sitting on a rusty glider, I spotted a nest on a low-lying limb of a nearby Red Oak. Frozen in the moment, I spied two mockingbirds swooping in to feed their young. The hungry chirping of the baby birds alerted me to their utter dependence on their parents provision. I watched with wonder the tips of their tiny yellow beaks spreading wide to receive their daily meal. During the next two weeks I marveled at this miraculous event. I witnessed the adult mockingbirds teaching their young to fly, demonstrating acrobatic skills with patience until their young mustered the courage to abandon the protection of their nest. Though saddened by their departure, I felt blessed to be present in these sacred moments of nature.

Every minute of every day God is with us. By learning to be aware and grateful for this gift so freely given, our life will take on new meaning and purpose and our hearts will expand to the glory of the moment in which we fully live in the infinite love of our Creator. The gift of time can never be replaced. It cannot be purchased or stored for the future, and it can never be regained once lost. It is the gift of the sacred now, a gift from God who instructs us to live it fully in its glory with joy and thanksgiving.

CHAPTER 12

"A Time to Sew"

In the breast of a bulb,
Is the promise of spring;
In the little blue egg,
Is a bird that will sing;
In the soul of a seed,
Is the hope of the sod;
In the heart of a child,
Is the kingdom of God.

WILLIAM L. STIDGER

LESSON 1

Hope

Laboring for days in my garden has me wondering if I can sustain the toil. I've pulled weeds for hours, and my neck, shoulders, and back are stiff. Seared from the sun's unrelenting rays, my body feels the drudgery of the labor and my spirit sinks. I confess to myself this may not be worth it. I ask myself why can't I be satisfied with a few potted plants adorning the front porch? Why must I torture myself each spring planting every unique shrub or whimsical flower I discover at the local nursery?

I discover in my doubt a bud of Hope; it whispers *one day I will bask in the beauty of a magnificent garden.* I discover my garden dreams give meaning to my existence. They strengthen my heart and beckon me to a deep desire that lies within. The bud starts to open, and my Hope blossoms. Something about the beauty of a garden sustains my vision, and I wonder if this "Eden dream" is the same dream God envisioned for His people?

Hope sustains us through trials and tribulations. It feeds our dreams and helps us carry on through poverty, disease, death, divorce, and disaster. Without Hope, our darkest hours would be meaningless. The essential Hope in God's garden lifts our spirits and replenishes our souls. It believes in a brighter future and all it has to offer. The joy of a new born baby, the exciting prospect of a new job, falling in love and getting married, are all symbols of Hope. Even in death's grip, we hope for everlasting life. Hope illuminates our darkest hours, protecting our hearts from fear and despair. When all else fails us, hope remains as a steadfast companion, encouraging us to not give up or give in.

> *"The LORD is my shepherd; I shall not want. He maketh me to lie down in green pastures; he leadeth me beside the still waters, he restores my soul...."*
>
> **PSALM 23:1-2 (KJV)**

Hope nourishes and encourages my soul during times of stress. It shepherds me to a calm place where my anxious fears are quieted. It brings me solace and comfort, allowing me to rest in green pastures of endless grace. Hope anticipates a positive outcome to whatever we struggle with. It carries no burden and makes no demands. The smallest Hope carries the potential of greatness, like an acorn's potential of becoming a majestic oak. Like the acorn, we carry the hope of becoming like our Redeemer, doing greater things than He.

> *"but those who hope in the LORD will renew their strength, They will soar on*

> *wings like eagles; they will run and not*
> *grow weary, they will walk and not*
> *be faint."*

ISAIAH 40:31 (NIV)

Hope trusts not in our own understanding, but in a higher power who strengthens us by clearing pathways, allowing the light to show us the way. Hope helps us to see things from a higher realm, opening our eyes to possibilities that would otherwise not be known to us. A world without hope reflects a cold harsh winter without promise of spring. With spirits anguished and empty, there is no refuge or strength, courage or peace. Hopelessness, like a menacing viper, revels in defeat, destruction, and despair, leaving fear in its wake. Hope promises we will defeat fear; it promises one day there will be no more hunger, or pain, or tears. It believes in all things and Hopes in all things (1 Corinthians 13:7)

"I Will Rise," one of my favorite contemporary Christian songs by Chris Tomlin, reflects the sentiment in 1 Corinthians 13:7. It talks about Jesus overcoming the grave and winning the victory against darkness. It further goes on to say that our own conquering of pain and sorrow will be at the end of our journey and we will rise on eagle's wings.

When the long hoped for Messiah was born, He heralded in a promise of new life with God. He taught lessons of hope, love, mercy, and grace, and forever changed history with this message. His crucifixion and resurrection symbolized hope in all its glory as

He defeated death by rising above it. Hope revealed in birth and hope revealed in death, like the seasons, renews itself in our hearts when we dream of greater things than we can ever imagine.

Hope heralds in spring with new life and abundance. It dances and rejoices in the beauty of the garden of our souls, where we trust and love our Creator who sustains us with His compassion and grace.

LESSON 2

Humility

"Humble yourselves in the sight of the Lord, and He shall exalt you."

JAMES 4:10 (ASV)

"Be completely humble and gentle; be patient bearing with one another in love."

EPHESIANS 4:2 (NIV)

"Live in harmony with one another. Do not be haughty, but associate with the lowly..."

ROMANS 12:16 (ESV)

There are over 25 Bible verses that address the virtue of humility and when we act nobly on this virtue, we glorify God by forsaking pride and humbling ourselves in all our interactions. Humility is not about thinking less of ourselves or running ourselves into the ground. Nor does humility keep silent when we need to speak up. Humility assumes the responsibility of maintaining a right view of ourselves in relationship to God and others. Equality, in the eyes of God, means we are not better or worse than anyone else; we are all sinners, and by maintaining that view in all of our interactions, we cloak ourselves in humility. We can assume therefore, that God made us exactly who we are for a reason, not better or worse than anyone else.

Humility's openness to ideas, advice, and criticism paves the way for spiritual growth, which recognizes our gifts as God given, rather than claiming them haughtily as our own. Living in harmony with others without being haughty and associating with all sorts of people, including the lowly, helps us acquire empathy and understanding of different life situations. Rather than beating our chests and proclaiming our righteousness, we fare better if we heed the lessons of Jesus Who taught that we should not proclaim our good deeds in public as the Pharisees did. The practice of humility involves praying in secluded places and giving charitably in private so we don't flaunt our spirituality in front of others to gain attention or praise. Our lives demonstrate humility when we follow the example of Jesus Who spent His life humbly serving crowds of unworthy sinners. Yet to acquire and maintain humility proves a challenging life-long endeavor of practice, patience, and prayer.

In my own life-long struggle with humility, I find myself wanting attention from others and being a bit self-absorbed and self-centered. It's no wonder, for I was born the "invisible" third child of a working-class family. There are hardly any baby pictures of me, no records of my existence, and few stories, other than

I had terrible colic. My parents, too busy trying to support three children, hardly noticed me and when they did it was because I was fighting for attention with my two older sisters. I came into this world screaming, and I've been trying to get noticed ever since! When my younger brother came along it was even worse, for I was no longer the baby, and he was celebrated as the long hoped for boy. In order to get attention, I had to adopt a personality that would hardly be considered humble. I was competitive, sarcastic, proud, and loud! How else could I make people acknowledge me?

As I grew in faith however, I realized these maladaptive traits needed to be replaced with something that resembled humility. I had a hard time understanding how this worked, because in most of my dealings with other people, the ones who displayed prideful behaviors seemed to get exactly what they wanted. To be humble felt weak, and weakness wasn't something I wanted to feel. However, as I grew closer to God, I soon realized that humility required great strength: strength to admit we are weak and fallible human beings and ask for help to do what is right in the eyes of God. Humility, I discovered, embodies the best of the human spirit: compassion, courage, gratitude, generosity, harmony, and understanding.

I discovered in my quest for humility that the world sadly lacks humanity, for the humanity of this world is dependent on our humility and there is little of that to be found these days. To this day I have never heard a sermon addressing this difficult subject. Many churches have budgets that exceed hundreds of thousands of dollars in order to keep the lights on, and at the same time, they give as little as ten percent of donations to charity. The mega churches with mega budgets hardly represent a humble carpenter, born in a stable, who spent His life serving widows and orphans. In today's modern culture of "just do it" and "there is no second best," we learn to "dress for success" and "grab for the gold." With slogans like these, it's no wonder our society struggles with the virtue of humility.

One could say that humility is the source of all virtue, whereas pride the source of all sin. Pride, the opposite of humility, is rampant in developed Western and European cultures. In America, many people view the modest homes of the seventies and eighties as too small, so they are purchasing monstrous dwellings averaging three to six thousand square feet, while at the same time, many poor live on the streets without food or shelter. Stores like Goodwill would have you believe they are charitable organizations, yet their CEO's make over five hundred thousand a year. Millions of people attend church to learn about the life of Jesus, yet His humility mystically eludes our souls and societies. With corporate greed on the rise, leaders in government cater to their donors while disregarding the needs of their people.

So how did Jesus, born in a stable, and dying on a wooden cross among thieves, become such a commanding spiritual influence? How did the humble carpenter riding through the streets on a donkey telling His disciples not to claim Him as the Messiah become so popular? We continue to indulge in the sins of arrogance, greed, and pride without counting the cost to humanity. Without humility, humanity's evolution barely eclipses the apes, and some scientists believe apes to possess more humility and compassion than the average man.

The daily practice of humility combats the sin of pride and challenges us to become more compassionate toward ourselves and others. In order to evolve, we do well to listen more than we speak and consider every living thing to have inherent and equal value as our own.

> *"God opposes the proud but shows favor to the humble."*
>
> JAMES 4:6 (NIV)

> *"When pride comes, then comes disgrace, but with humility comes wisdom."*
>
> PROVERBS 11:2 (NIV)

> *This is what the Lord says: "Let not the wise boast of their wisdom or the strong boast of their strength or the rich boast of their riches."*
>
> JEREMIAH 9:23 (NIV)

> *Humility is not about thinking less of ourselves; it's about thinking about ourselves less*
>
> (C.S. LEWIS)

Humility's nemesis, pride, has over thirty Bible verses. God opposes pride because pride boasts about self, lives for self, and is absorbed with self. Some of the richest and most prideful nations in history were led by self-righteous leaders. Because of their pride, their nations fell into destruction and despair, whereas leaders who have displayed great courage and humility have risen to become history's heroes. Even though some of these heroes met untimely deaths, their stories of great humility live on. Gandhi, Abraham Lincoln, Dr. Martin Luther King, Mother Teresa, and many others displayed the qualities of humbleness. Each of them found their strength and convictions in a higher power and served their fellow man with grace, compassion, truth, and love. They stood up courageously for the poor, meek and marginalized, and never wavered in their commitment for justice in the world. As Gandhi taught, if we were to spend more time understanding one another, and less time judging or criticizing, we would achieve peace around the world because humility begins in the heart, with nothing to prove and everything to offer. These powerful and humble leaders of spiritual justice changed the course of humanity, at least for a while. It is our turn to pick up where they left off, to practice humility in all our daily interactions, to teach lessons in humility by example, and to embody the lessons of our Lord Jesus Christ, Who with great humility and compassion died for us, so that we may live.

CHAPTER 13

"A Time to Dance"

Dance is the hidden language of the soul of the body

MARTHA GRAHAM

LESSON 1

Joy Divine

Be it a flock of geese flying home for winter, or a child's tender kiss, joy is all around us, and God calls us to rejoice in it. In the midst of petty daily struggles however, joy can seem elusive. Yet right underneath our disgruntled noses, joy flirts with us, hoping to catch our attention. This morning, I struggled with writing about joy and heard faint music playing in the background. Engrossed in my task, I missed God's message in the same way many of us struggle with our problems when all the while God's simple solution was in our midst. This morning while stewing over what to write, I suddenly became aware of the music playing in the background. The "aha moment" was so obvious, I started laughing! The song playing was Ludwig Van Beethoven's, ninth symphony, "Ode to Joy," (words written by Henry Van Dyke.) This inspiring symphony begins with "Joyful, Joyful, We Adore Thee." God was speaking to me, and I in my human fog wasn't listening. The very minute I acknowledged God's helpful hand in my writing, words started pouring into my head, and I wrote them down as fast as I could. Like so many other moments in my life, God was speaking loud and clear, and I wasn't listening. But this time I caught it just in time. I suppose in a way this is my "Ode to Joy." Thank you Ludwig, (and God)!

Rejoice in the Lord! The God of glory, the God of love. Let the multitude of God's gifts fill your soul. Let your hearts unfold like flowers to His redeeming love. Let the sun warm your hearts with endless joy. Feel the love of the world surround you and melt the clouds of sadness away. Giver of all miracles fill us with the light of day. The life of creation surrounds us, passionate unbroken praise. Fragrant flowers, singing bird, golden meadow or flashing sea. Oh! miracle of love, we rejoice in Thee.
Life-Giver of strength and love, ever blessing, ever blest. You are the wellspring of the joy of living, an ocean depth of happy rest! Thou art our Father, and our brother; teach us how to love each other. Abiding in the love of Thine, lift us to the Joy divine.
Let magnitudes of mortals join in happy song, with stars in heaven's band. Let the Lord reign over all the earth, binding heart to heart and hand to hand. Let the bread of heaven feed our souls, as we march with endless praise. Victors in

the midst of strife, we sing to the end
of days.
Oh! Mighty Warrior, release my fears,
forge rivers of mercy through my tears.
Glory in truth, my soul rejoice, To you,
my God I lift my voice. Sing praise to
the Son, the risen King. Let the trumpets
sound and the Church bells ring!
Salvation's throne, your glorious call, Lift
angels high, my All in All!
Heaven's shield and mercy's wing, to Thee
O Lord our praises sing!
Joy to the world, Eden divine, sunlit from
Heaven for all mankind.
Prepare ye our hearts for earth's new
King; let the realms of Heaven and
Nature sing!

LESSON 2

Lord of the Dance

One of my favorite hymns, *The Lord of the Dance*, written by Sydney Carter, is an adaptation of an old English carol called *Tomorrow Shall Be My Dancing Day*, which tells the Gospel story in the first-person voice of Jesus. The song portrays Jesus' life and mission as a dance.

> *I danced in the morning when the*
> *world was begun*
> *And I danced in the moon and the stars*
> *and the sun,*
> *And I came down from heaven and*
> *I danced on earth:*
> *At Bethlehem I had my birth.*
>
> *Chorus: Dance, then, wherever you*
> *may be,*
> *I am the Lord of the dance, said he,*
> *And I'll lead you all, wherever you*
> *may be,*
> *And I'll lead you all in the dance, said he.*

Dancing with God celebrates all living beings.

This celebration dance taught by our Creator, helps us stretch beyond mortal limits to reach our greatest potential by developing compassion, forgiveness, courage, and love. Choreographed to the beat of God's heart, life becomes a celebratory dance each and every time we move to His beat. God urges us to set in motion the intention to be truthful and purposeful in all our movements, and by doing so, we take steps toward healing in a wounded world. Healing occurs when we achieve peace with God, our neighbors, ourselves, and the world.

> *I danced for the scribe, and the Pharisee,*
> *But they would not dance, and they*
> *wouldn't follow me;*
> *I danced for the fisherman, for James*
> *and John;*
> *They came with me, and the dance*
> *went on.*

When we dance the peace-dance, we are offered a chance to experience God's spiritual gifts by listening to the music of our souls and dancing to that music. If we ignore the music, we ignore the Composer who inspires us. We must be attentive to Him, and allow Him to lead while we follow. When God calls us to the dance, we must respond with open hearts and minds if we are to experience the many gifts He offers us. Once we understand this pattern of call and response, we learn to listen to our soul's music, and our lives begin to change. Things begin to align themselves in a way that feels right, and we know instinctively we are in step with God.

> *I danced on the Sabbath and I cured
> the lame;*
> *The holy people said it was a shame.*
> *They whipped and they stripped, and they
> hung me high*
> *And they left me there on a cross to die.*

Dancing with God is not always easy. Sometimes we experience pain for the sake of truth and righteousness. Sometimes we are hurt during the dance because people we thought we could count on, forsake us. We feel battered and bruised and consider giving up the dance.

> *I danced on a Friday when the sky
> turned black*
> *It's hard to dance with a devil on
> your back*
> *They buried my body and they thought
> I'd gone*
> *But I am the dance, and I still go on.*

Sometimes the world we know collapses around us, and everything turns black. We begin to fear and feel as though we are doing everything right, yet nothing seems to be working. It becomes difficult to judge whether our steps are the right ones; we feel out of sync, awkward, and start to become skeptical. The music in our souls seems in discord, and we find ourselves questioning whether this dance with God is worth it. The weight of darkness surrounds us, and we feel buried in our sorrows. This necessary part of the dance teaches us that even in the midst of darkness, we must trust God and still go on.

> *They cut me down and I leapt up high;*
> *I am the life that will never, never die*
> *I'll live in you if you live in me:*
> *I am the Lord of the dance, said he.*

As a matter of faith, God raises us up to rejoice in the dance that has been so beautifully choreographed for us. The Lord's dance is a dance about life, struggle, resurrection, and transformation. Let us make every day a celebration and dance of our new life in Jesus, Lord of the Dance!

> *Dance, then, wherever you may be,*
> *I am the Lord of the dance, said he,*
> *And I'll lead you all, wherever you*
> *may be,*
> *And I'll lead you all in the dance, said he.*

CHAPTER 14

"A Time to Gather Stones"

The man who removes a mountain,
Begins by carrying away small stones.

CHINESE PROVERB

Strength

When we have mustered all our physical and mental strength and can no longer endure the hardships in our lives, God gives us strength of spirit. Praying for strength and acknowledging our weakness before God is a humble act of submission that invites our Protector into the deepest regions of our soul to strengthen and heal us. With God's power and love, we can overcome whatever life's trials and tribulations throw at us. Like the seeds of wildflowers scattered in the wind, we land on hard times and struggle to blossom. But if you've ever closely examined wildflowers, you might notice they grow and bloom in the strangest of places. Some grow out of cracks in rock or asphalt while others grow despite little water or nutrients. Much like the wildflowers, we have been scattered and grow in less than ideal conditions. We survive neglect, tragedy, illness, abuse, abandonment, and the absence of love. Yet despite these hardships, with God's help we flourish like wildflowers.

In gardening, a method called *hardening off* helps a plant acclimate to its surroundings. A plant which has been protected in a greenhouse is gradually exposed to harsher conditions in order to help it survive. Otherwise the shock of the environment would be too great, and the plant would die. God has a similar method to help us endure hardships, so that we do not become overwhelmed by them. Little by little as we develop our faith, we learn to trust God's provision in good times and in bad so that we may become stronger. Our strength of spirit comes directly from God, and when called upon, becomes the birthplace of our divine power and resourcefulness. Without God's strength, we would quickly be defeated by the dark forces that surround us daily. When we recognize the enormity of God's power, and tap into its strength, like the wildflowers, we not only survive, but thrive!

Our frail human nature, weak and insecure, will certainly be tested over and over, sometimes reaching extremes we feel are too great to bear. Yet each time we call on God, we overcome these obstacles and demonstrate His strength and power to others. In this way weakness becomes our strength because our weaknesses, though exposed, becomes witness to God's love and strength working through us. "...My grace is sufficient for you, for power is made perfect in weakness." 2 Corinthians 12:9 (NIV) Therefore, exposing our weaknesses, frailties, and fears to God, through prayer, provides a pathway to our heart, and instead of building walls around our imperfections, we open ourselves up to healing. Healing, whether mental, spiritual or physical, strengthens us so that we may serve others. We begin this journey by declaring our personal vulnerabilities and needs to God. When we pray for strength, God provides it; when we pray for forgiveness, He forgives; when we are ill, God heals; and when we need love, He supplies it. There is literally nothing God won't do when it comes to strengthening and supporting us, if we have faith and believe in His power. God's limitless strength provides limitless opportunities, and those opportunities pave the way for us and others to live in hope rather than fear.

> *"So do not fear, for I am with you; do not be dismayed, for I am your God, I will strengthen you and help you; I will uphold you with my righteous right hand."*

ISAIAH 41:10 (NIV)

Now more than ever, we need God's strength to stand up for truth and righteousness in a world full of fear. We need it in our homes, schools, churches, and government. We need it to defy those who would oppress and dismiss the frail and weak of our society. And we need it to build a more peaceful and loving world. Strength, along with courage, in the name of God's love and truth, guide us toward a better world as we take refuge in the arms of our Savior and loose our fears.

> *"The LORD is my light and my salvation; whom shall I fear? The Lord is the stronghold of my life; of whom shall I*

be afraid?"

PSALM 27:1 (**NIV**)

As president Roosevelt used to say, "We have nothing to fear but fear itself." He knew all too well that fear can create mass hysteria and sometimes even violence. Fear divides people, families, friends, churches, and synagogues. It is used by others to control. This is why it is wise to put God in charge of our lives, especially when consumed by fear. 1 John 4:18 says, "There is no fear in love, but perfect love casts out fear. For fear has to do with punishment, and whoever fears has not been perfected in love." (ESV) When we love God, ourselves, and others, we are perfected in a way that builds a fortress around our hearts to keep out fear. By doing so, we allow God in and keep fear out. Who better than God to fight our spiritual battles? Who better than the light of pure love to cast out the darkness of fear and doubt? As we move through our spiritual journey, remember God is always near to fight our battles. All we must do is ask in the fullness of faith, and we shall receive the grace of God's strength and courage.

CHAPTER 15

"A Time to Embrace"

Nature is the living visible garment of God

JOHANN WOLFGANG
VON GOETHE

LESSON 1

Seasons

*For everything there is a season, and a
time for every matter under heaven:*

*A time to be born, a time to die;
A time to plant, and a time to pluck what
was planted;
A time to kill, and a time to heal;
A time to break down, and a time to
build up;
A time to weep, a time to laugh;
A time to mourn, and a time to dance;
A time to cast away stones, and a time to
gather stones together;
A time to embrace, and a time to refrain
from embracing;
A time to seek, and a time to lose;
A time to keep, and a time to cast away;
A time to tear, and a time to sew;
A time to keep silent, and a time to speak;
A time to love, a time to hate;
A time for war, and a time for peace.*

ECCLESIASTES 3:1-8 (ESV)

The seasons of the spiritual life come and go just like the seasons of nature. There are seasons of change, seasons of learning, seasons of being tested, seasons of mourning, seasons of growth, and seasons of light. In every season in which we live, we can count on God to give us strength when we are weak, love when we feel hate, and forgiveness when we sin. If we pay attention to our spiritual seasons, we will recognize that they unfold, turn, change, and grow just as the seasons of nature do.

In every season there are lessons to be learned, and we grow and learn more about God as we study the teachings of His Word. The Old Testament reminds us of our Christian lineage, God's commandments, and promises made and kept. The New Covenant teaches us the riches of relationship to ourselves and others. It teaches us to love one another and turn the other cheek. Christ teaches us to follow our hearts rather than rigid law. Through the seasons of childhood, adulthood, marriage, divorce, and death, we learn Jesus is always present. He walks side by side with us, carries our burdens, and catches us when we fall. When walking with Christ, we learn about becoming laborers in His vineyard and producing fruit worthy of God's kingdom. Through sweat, toil, and tears, we learn to reap the harvest of wisdom in a world that is severely lacking. We learn that Christ came not only to save us, but to teach us. He is the Master, and we, the students.

The growing season of our spiritual life involves change, and change is difficult. It often happens in conjunction with the learning season. As we learn and grow, we begin to change. Growing into spiritual beings, however, isn't automatic just because we acquire knowledge. We must move, stretch, and grow often to the point of being uncomfortable because change and growth are sometimes painful. If we've been deceiving ourselves and others the whole of our lives, it is difficult to feel the pain of our destructive and dysfunctional behavior and move beyond it.

We know we have to change, but our spirits resist because we want to stay in the comfort zone of what is familiar, even if it hurts us. The season of growth and change feels like we are emerging out of a dark cocoon, in which we have been trapped for a long time. Coming into the light is difficult because it feels unfamiliar. For this reason, we must be gentle with ourselves and not push too hard. At the same time, we must persevere because the spiritual rewards are worth it. In recognizing where we need to grow spiritually, we learn that when something is new, it feels uncomfortable to us. This is our body's natural resistance to our homeostasis, or something we have done for a very long time. The season of growth and change then involves breaking down and building up. We must allow God to break down the walls that prevent us from spiritual wholeness and rebuild them with His love.

Of course, the most difficult season of change comes when we experience a life entering or leaving our world. The birth of a child is miraculous, but our whole life changes because we must adjust to a new life and give up old ways. Similarly, when we marry, we must change and adapt to the person we love and work together to create harmony within the union. If one person insists on their own way, or tries to control the other, or becomes too dependent, the union fails. And this leads to the season of mourning. When we lose a child, a mother, father, or spouse, we mourn and weep and feel deeply the pain of our loss. With Jesus at our side we find the courage to go on with our lives, in spite of our pain. The season of grief has no end. Grief is different for everyone. Some grieve for a lifetime, and some move on. But either way, loss of a loved one is painful. We have shared our hopes, dreams, desires, and fears, and connected with them through the divine union of relationship. In these difficult seasons, God watches over us, comforts us, and heals us.

The cycles of spiritual growth mirror the seasons' ever-changing moods with each person's journey, repeating these cycles over and over again. One may experience the dark winter days of death more than once in a life, or several joyful births. One can even experience both joy and despair in the same season. But as we cycle through dark and light filled days there are always spiritual gifts to be thankful for. Moments of joy, love, comfort, and peace await us if we stay connected to our Creator and accept that "this too shall pass."

As we experience these seasons, we come to realize that in every season's folds lie the potential for us to come closer to God, whether to guide and protect us, to laugh and celebrate with us, or to weep and suffer with us. In the seasons of life, God matters because we matter to Him. We are not alone. His blessings, when measured by our time, are infinite. We may not see them through the fog of our fears, but they are there. Whether in winter's darkness, fall's bounty, spring's hope, or summer's malaise, we learn to weep, laugh, mourn, and dance. We learn it takes time to heal, and that life's seasons go on.

Spiritual Discipline

In the dictionary, *discipline* is defined as *a training expected to produce a specific type of pattern or behavior, especially training that produces moral or mental improvement.* However, when I think of obedience and discipline, I think of a loss of freedom. That is why spiritual discipline is difficult for me. When I became a Christian, I did not realize it entailed a lifelong process of training and discipline. Part of the training includes understanding that life is a series of choices that help us grow according to God's will instead of our own. When we choose our own will, our lives become as chaotic as our feelings, which come and go depending on which way life's winds blow. Like a tumbleweed, our feelings toss and turn while aimlessly roaming in a desert and searching for a place to land. Choosing God's will over our own helps us manage our feelings and ground them in His authority, which provides guidance for living our lives. Without grounding in God, we may only love when we feel like it, or work when the mood strikes us. Discipline provides the will to do what is right in the eyes of God. When our thoughts are on God and what He wants, we gain new freedom because we are no longer hostage to our whimsical and unpredictable feelings. God grounds us in His reality rather than our own, which gives us a joyful purpose as we turn our discipline into action in everything we say and do.

The word *discipline* is derived from the word *disciple*. To be disciples of Christ, we are called to discipline ourselves through the teachings of Christ. When we stray from this, we become vulnerable to being lost in the darkness of the world. When we discipline ourselves to live according to God's will, our lives embody a sense of calm and peace. In calm and peace, we regain our freedom, for nothing in this world can separate us from the love of God. By practicing spiritual discipline, we keep this connection alive and well, and in so doing, pave the way to love others the way God loves us.

The joy-filled journey of spiritual discipline is a road less traveled, for most of us want to rule our own lives. We search for happiness, but it becomes elusive as we try to control our lives by choosing whatever we think will gratify us in the moment. Without consideration for others, we choose false images of satisfaction for what we think will make us happy. For example, we may choose the love of money over relationships, or idleness over hard work. We choose to do what we want to do, when we want to do it. Imagine if this were God's way. Imagine if God chose to let the sun rise only when He felt like it, or love only when the mood was right for Him. Spiritual discipline calls us to be more God-like. It calls us to give love and attention to others even when we would rather not. It calls us to move beyond ourselves and become the hands and feet of God in this fallen world. In so doing we help create a stable and predictable environment for others to grow in love.

God's way is not always easy; it invokes a high moral standard of faith to become the foundation of our lives. As fallible humans, our quest to become righteous can easily morph into spiritual pride. Therefore, our goal should not be spiritual or moral perfection (a fallacy in itself), but to assume a stance of humility that speaks to others in a way that expresses that we too are weak and stumbling on the rocky road of righteousness. Spiritual discipline guides us to be Christ-like, therefore we must not assume we are above or below others. In God's eyes we are all equal, both saint and sinner.

This is why Paul tells Timothy: "Have nothing to do with irreverent, silly myths. Rather train yourself for godliness; for while bodily training is of some value, godliness is of value in every way, as it holds promise for the present life and also for the life to come. 1 Timothy 4:7-8 (ESV)

Through the discipline of daily prayer, faith, study, and action, we train ourselves and develop the habit of connecting to God and others. Prayer is the daily bread that feeds our souls; it calms our minds and clears away the debris that obstructs our connection to God and others. Prayer is how we talk to God. When we pray, God listens. Prayer may include meditation, confession, petition, or movement or voice prayer such as dancing or singing. Faith, barricades the doors to fear and worry which cloud our thinking and keep us trapped in a cycle of anxiety. Faith brings all the benefits of salvation into our lives, "For it is by grace you have been saved. through faith- and this is not from yourselves, it is a gift of God." Ephesians 2:8 (NIV)

Faith is an active belief that God is in control. We may practice our faith anytime and anywhere. Faith becomes a port in the storm in times of strife, it helps guide and comfort us and will never let us down. Fasting is a spiritual practice of faith, for it invites a spiritual dependence on God, rather than dependence on earthly sustenance. Studying the Word helps us know God and becomes the roadmap to living our lives in accordance with God's will, for through study we gain the knowledge to live in the spirit of righteousness. By seeking the light of God's Word, our path is lit so that we may follow it to find our purpose.

> *"Thy word is a lamp unto my feet and a light unto my path"*
>
> **PSALM 119:105 (KJV)**

Action, the worker-bee of faith, includes, but is not limited to, generosity, disciple-making, service, and celebration. Action may be as simple as forgiveness, or as powerful as helping to rebuild lives after a tornado or hurricane. Action moves us to give, evangelize, and help others.

> *Giving: "...It is more blessed to give than to receive."*
>
> **ACTS 20:35 (NIV)**

Evangelize: "Therefore go and make disciples of all nations..."

MATTHEW 28:19 (**NIV**)

Help others: "...serve one another humbly in love..."

GALATIANS 5:13 (**NIV**)

Without action or fruit of our faith, prayer, faith, and study have no meaning or purpose. Conversely, action without prayer, faith, and study become a self-centered endeavor, void of God. Spiritual discipline teaches us to become the hands and feet of God. By developing good habits of spiritual discipline, we become apprentices to Jesus, Who walked the human path to know and ease human suffering.

Ultimately, our glory and freedom come from the discipline of living and serving God's truth in the light of love. Every day in God's kingdom becomes a practice of discipline, not as harsh submission to oppressive and authoritative figures, but as a calling and desire to be more like God and serve His people with love.

LESSON 3

Willing Acceptance

Every morning I loosely plan my day by compiling a list of chores and projects that need to be accomplished. These may include responsibilities pertaining to my home, children, church, and work. The tasks are prioritized according to their importance, and by weeks end I feel good if I have succeeded in completing them. But more often than not, God has compiled a different list of which I was not aware. My children or husband may ask me to do something I had not planned, or just as I sit down to write, the phone rings, and it's my mother wanting to chat. The more I resist these annoyances, the more I feel the tug between my will and God's because God's plans usually include giving to, relating to, or sacrificing for others. The negative emotions I feel are real, and I grumble at the diversion from my well laid plans. However, if I accept these alterations as an opportunity for growth, the inner-conflict I feel is replaced with a peaceful willing acceptance.

Adopting the lesson to accept God's will over my own did not happen overnight. I, being a mover and shaker, set out to accomplish my goals with all the gusto of a freight train. Basically, I blow my horn for everyone to get out of the way, and off I go. Yet, by succumbing to the will of God over my own, I find the spiritual outcome enlightening. Instead of the good feeling I get from a job well done, which is about me, I am alerted to a higher power who lets me know His plans are better. His lessons are lessons in love rather than achievement. And those lessons teach me about myself and my values in relationship to others.

When I open the door to my heart and accept this willingly, I begin to understand the value of self-sacrifice over self-indulgence. Also, I have witnessed that God has my back in every situation, whether I stubbornly reject what He offers or accept with an open heart. However, when I fight His will over my own, I experience an internal battle of reality versus my vision, which may or may not materialize. This doesn't mean I sit back and do nothing, although sometimes that's what God calls me to do. It means that I accept whatever setbacks or diversions oppose my will as a Higher Power calling me in a different direction. Sometimes the call is to *"Be still, and know that I am God; ..." Psalm 46:10 (NIV)* Other times I feel God saying to me, "Stand back, and let the Master work." In these moments I laugh because who more than God knows my stubborn will and how much I fight to stay in control. When I willingly accept God's plan and timing over my own, I learn to live by spiritual guidance instead of my stubborn will. I learn to listen to God's inner voice in my soul. Discord arises when my self-will is not aligned with God's will. When I find myself filled with negative emotions or resistance,

I'm not allowing God to lead.

> *"Come to me, all you who are weary and burdened, and I will give you rest. Take my yoke upon you and learn from me, for I am gentle and humble in heart, and you will find rest for your souls. For my yoke is easy and my burden is light."*

MATTHEW 11:28-30 (NIV)

These verses from Matthew comfort me by letting me know I don't have to be a freight train to serve God. I don't have to drive myself to exhaustion trying to please others or reach some earthly illusion of perfection. When I accept God's will, I am in a Holy, safe place waiting for instruction from my Redeemer. It means I willingly accept God's perfect timing over my own, even if that means doing nothing. I once asked my spiritual advisor, "How do I know if the instruction or vision I have is from God?" She said simply, "If it's from God, it's good!"

When I began to write, I shared my spiritual insights with a group of women I met with every Sunday. It wasn't until I received positive feedback from these women that I considered turning my writings into a book. They encouraged my writing and suggested I send them to the "Esprit," an Episcopal monthly publication. Feeling a bit nervous and exposed, I took the chance, and within a month my writing had been published. Several church members who read it expressed how much they liked the article and how meaningful it was. My close friend asked me if she could share my writings with some co-workers who needed some spiritual guidance. My point here is not to brag about myself, but to acknowledge God was leading me down a path I had never considered. Had I been closed-minded to His will, I might not have had the courage to share my writing with my friends.

Even though I worked very hard writing every day for a year and was excited about this new journey, it didn't take long for doubt to settle in. I started questioning. *How can I be sure God wants me to write this book? How can I be sure my ego isn't wanting to be stroked for my talent?* Then I faced stumbling blocks when my computer crashed, and I lost my writings. I went through depression after my first marriage ended, and I could not write. I shelved my writing for years and convinced myself it was a lovely testament to my faith that my children might find after my death. The writings, forever stalled, remained dormant. Then one day I decided to look at them again. *They aren't bad,* I told myself. Then the voice in my head told me to finish what I had started. I questioned again, *why now?* And I heard the voice saying, "You have a story to tell." I realized in that moment that the story was not mine and never had been. The story was God's.

When I first started writing, I felt God directing me, but soon my ego-centric self, took over, and I envisioned someday I'd be a great writer, and people would look up to me as a wise spiritual guru. Thankfully this aggrandizement didn't last too long, and I realized that this time I wanted to do this for God. I wanted to let people know how much God had done for me in my life and continues to do so. I thought to myself, *if I could just help one person with this writing, the hours, heartaches, setbacks, and struggles would be worth it.* My freight train was back on track and in full steam, only this time it was not me; I felt God was the Conductor. This time I had a real purpose to tell God's story as I experienced it. Writing has become my discipline, my work, and my savior. It has helped me in ways I may never fully understand. I have healed from the pain of my childhood because I could tell my story when no else one cared to listen. I am still healing from a broken marriage, and writing helps me lay it out in black and white where I can clearly see the role God plays in my life. My story's not over, I have much more to tell, and many more books to write. Writing has become my discipline, my work, and my salvation all because I willingly accepted God's call.

CHAPTER 16

"A Time to Keep Silent"

Prayer is the soul's sincere desire,
Uttered or unexpressed;
The motion of a hidden fire,
That trembles in the breast.
Prayer is the burden of a sigh,
The falling of a tear,
The upward glancing of an eye,
When none but God is near.

JAMES MONTGOMERY

LESSON 1

Prayer

Prayer existed thousands of years before the Pony Express, telegraph, modern cell phones, texting, e-mail and Twitter. When praying, there are no wires, no dropped-calls, and no one else listening. Prayers are completely confidential. If you dial God's number through prayer, He will answer. God is standing by, 24 hours a day, seven days a week, waiting patiently for us to call on Him.

The sad news is that even though God is available to us 24 hours a day, many western religious institutions reserve prayer for Sunday services only. We foolishly assume communion with God once a week will keep us spiritually fulfilled. Rather than making time in our day for quiet reflective prayer or meditation, we're trapped on the treadmill of earthly tasks from the moment we wake until we plop our heads down on a pillow at night. We're left bewildered as to why we feel drained and disconnected from God and others, yet we don't have the time or energy to figure out why.

Caught up in worldly distractions, we often don't even realize something is missing until tragedy strikes. Not until then do we feel the emptiness of a spiritual connection to God and seek to find restitution with Him in hopes that God will relieve our suffering. What we have failed to realize is that making space for God in our daily lives brings peace to our homes, marriages, workplaces, schools, and churches. God loves us and wants to have a relationship with us. When we cultivate this relationship through prayer and faith, our lives change, and we begin to recognize the void we've been feeling can never be filled with anything earthly. Nothing replaces a relationship with God and prayer is the conduit which gives us a direct line to the Supreme Counselor, Teacher, Healer, Lover and Friend.

In monasteries around the world, cloisters of brothers and sisters gather to meditate and pray. In the beginning of the third century AD, the desert fathers and desert mothers were Christian hermits and monks who spent their days in desert cave dwellings praying and meditating in silence. They committed themselves to this lifestyle in order to grow closer to God. In Islam, prayer is woven five times into their daily lives in the same way westerners might take coffee breaks. The average worker stops production and travels to the Mosque for meditation and prayer. Years ago, I saw something unusual near the interstate where I lived that impressed me. A middle-eastern man parked his car on the side of the road and began praying. At first glance, I thought he was having car trouble. My inclination was to stop and help him, but as I came closer, I noticed he was holding a book and bowing repeatedly toward the Eastern sky. Astounded at the sight, I tried to imagine an American stopping on the interstate to spend quality time in prayer and although I occasionally pray while I drive, I've never taken the time to stop on the road and pray. This occurrence helped me understand how important the need for prayer is to maintaining peace in our everyday lives.

Opening our hearts to God in prayer, helps us feel closer to the Divine Spirit Who helps us experience inner peace in our fallen world. Listening is part of communication and therefore part of prayer. In so doing, we gain spiritual wisdom as we practice listening with our whole being. When we ask, or communicate our issues, our hearts open to fully understand God's purpose for our lives, as God leads us on a journey that produces the fruits of love, joy, peace, goodness, kindness, gentleness, faithfulness, and self-control. When asked faithfully in prayer, these fruits are given as a gift to be used in the fallen world in which we live.

> *"So I say to you: Ask and it will be given to you, seek and you will find, knock and the door will be opened to you."*
>
> **LUKE 11:9 (NIV)**

A healthy prayer life, like a healthy garden, is a healing experience, it opens our hearts and minds to God's holy Word. Prayer may include asking for forgiveness, being grateful, seeking answers to our struggles, or simply knocking to see where God is in relationship to us. It may include meditation, dance, song, or service to others. There is really no place we cannot pray. Some people pray while cleaning house, others make a special altar with candles and mementos. When we fill our spiritual garden with prayer, it manifests divine possibilities and allows us to flourish in the light of Gods' love.

Many of my deepest prayers occur when walking in my garden. Filled with awe and wonder, I marvel at the beauty of God's creation. I mourn over plants perished and hope in new life to come. Weather permitting, I stroll outside each morning, communicating with God and my plants. As I am caretaker of my garden, I sense the similarities of God as Caretaker of my soul. We communicate with one another, asking how we are doing and whether or not we need anything. As I examine the plants looking for signs of disease, God looks for signs of spiritual dis-ease in me, encouraging me to see my life with His eyes, not my own. I feel at one with God in my garden. While breathing in the fresh dewy air, I walk with God and absorb the beauty around me, all the while thanking Him for the warm sunshine, the soft breeze, and the dandelion puff balls that I delight in blowing. I pull weeds and pray, asking God lots of questions and He answers. While the birds are busy chirping, I wonder if they're praying too. As I meander with God, I praise Him for the awe and wonder in my life and mourn with Him over my losses. Then, I discover that part of prayer, which is most important, listening.

If I am listening well, God signals me. He lets me know what I need, when I need it. If I am listening well, He warns me, encourages me, or places obstacles in my path to tell me to wait. If I am not listening well, He continues to nudge me gently and relentlessly until I hear. If I find myself facing similar trials over and over again, it may be God telling me I need change, or to pull a few weeds in my soul.

Coming to God in prayer can be as simple and straightforward as walking in my garden. Prayers of thanksgiving praise God for all He has done for us. Writing our prayers as letters, or journaling, is an effective way to clear the debris out of our minds and get to the heart of our concerns. Meditative prayer, or silent retreats, teach us the truth. Corporate, or community, prayer allows us to connect with others in ways we otherwise would not.

No matter our style, God will answer our prayers in the fullness of our faith. Hardly intimidated by our needs, God wants us to be filled with the Holy Spirit of peace and the grace of His loving Son. Through Jesus, God wants us to surrender our lives to His Word of truth and grace. This mystic communication involves laying aside our ego so that God assumes absolute power in our lives. As we give up ourselves to Him through prayer, we become reborn into a spirit of love and everlasting light. (John 3:3)

No one knows physically how prayer works, but there have been countless testimonies from believers and non-believers alike as to the miracles of prayer. All around the world, prayer groups have been formed in hospitals, churches, and on the internet, praying for those with serious illnesses, death, or other tragedies. In recent years it has become more common to find doctors and surgeons praying over their patients. (I know which doctor I want on my side!) Some believe it is a type of bio-feedback. Others, who have been the recipient of miracles, testify they felt a spiritual presence in their midst. One does not have to witness the power of prayer to know that it works.

God is always waiting for us to come to Him in prayer; the lines are open. Nothing is insignificant to Him. We are loved unconditionally by Him. The more we take time out of our harried lives to pray with God and the more we listen, the more we get to know and love Him. He infuses our lives with new meaning and purpose, allowing us to do His work in a fallen world.

CHAPTER 17

"A Time to Love"

God is love;
and he that dwelleth in love
dwelleth in God,
And God in him.

1 JOHN 4:16 KJV

LESSON 1

Grace

The redeeming quality of God's grace brings salvation and transformation. It moves us to love one another and rejoice, as we act in accordance with God's will. Written in 1779 by John Newton, the hymn "Amazing Grace" tells us that even though we have been through many dangers, toils, and snares, "it is grace that brought us safe thus far, and grace will lead us home." Like the song, in every story worth telling, grace reveals itself as the divine presence in life. Joy, sorrow, love, and death are universal themes; no one escapes them. Woven into our stories, grace appears often and in various forms. Sometimes grace appears like a beautiful bride, but more often grace reveals herself in the quiet moments of a sunset or garden.

God's grace, a gift which inspires the action of divine love, enables God's power and spiritual healing to manifest in our lives. Crystallized in the realms of heaven, grace, offered through the mercy and love of Jesus Christ, inspires us toward virtuous impulses and imparts strength to endure life's trials and tribulations. In the Hebrew tradition the word *grace* means *favor*, and God shows favor by giving us glimpses of His redeeming love in a way that blesses us beyond measure. To sense the presence of God in all we see, say, and do, transforms us into divine beings of grace.

Often entering our hearts like a radiant bride to a wedding, God's grace is worth celebrating. Grace opens our eyes to the majesty of the rising and setting sun, the miracle of birth or the peace we feel in the passing of a suffering loved one. In the most difficult of circumstances, God's grace becomes a balm which soothes us in times of need, heals our wounded hearts, absolves our sins, and repairs the afflictions of our souls. Fueled with light and love, the celebration of amazing grace in our spiritual journey reminds us we are not alone.

The grace of God, as manifested in redemption, inspires a renewed spiritual diligence in all our interactions with others. Significant to the grace of our spiritual healing, Christ's lessons teach us to love and accept God, ourselves, and others so that we may be redeemed. These relationships are the training grounds for spiritual growth and take on profound meaning when permeated with the grace of God. Beyond our closest relationships, we move toward grace by mirroring Christ's devotion to the forgotten peoples of the earth: the poor, destitute, and war-torn children; the beggar on the street; and the single mother or father struggling to raise children. Each time we accept God's grace and will over our own, the angels celebrate the homecoming of our soul.

> *"My son, do not despise the chastening
> of the Lord, nor detest His correction; For
> whom the Lord loves He corrects, just as a
> father, the son in whom He delights."*

PROVERBS 3:11-12 (NKJV)

Rather than ranking others according to their attributes or demanding perfection, our Heavenly Father re-forms us into disciples worthy of His Kingdom. It's a blessing that clothes us in the spirit of humility where we learn from a compassionate King Who lifts the broken from the depths of despair to the realms of glory. Grace's redemption manifests in reformation. God's grace moves human hearts into becoming forgiving, kind, and merciful beings. Like a diamond in the rough, God sees the divine potential of every human. He sees what lies beneath the surface of our course exterior and chisels away our rough edges. The divine Gem-Cutter chips away our pride and helps us see the imperfections of our souls. He shapes us into brilliant specimens which reflect the light and love of His Son, Jesus Christ. His love for us, shown through grace which He imparts on this pain and joy-filled journey, transforms us beyond ourselves so that we are available to a world that cries for more peace, love, and understanding.

Each time we come to God asking for grace, a transformation takes place. We find refuge, strength, and mercy to carry us through our weary days. When coming to God looking for grace, we must come to Him boldly and proclaim our needs. (Hebrews 4:16) We must lay at the feet of God all that burdens us so that we may find comfort and peace. By doing so, we are reborn into new life, a life filled with meaning and purpose which we never imagined could be possible. No longer paralyzed by imagined limitations, we leap and bound with the infusion of God's inexhaustible energy and the promise of a new life in the wonders of grace.

Grace, our salvation by faith (Ephesians 2:8-9), frees us from ourselves and leads us down a path of spiritual enlightenment where our vision of the world changes. No longer do we see the problems of the world as unsolvable, for grace brings hope. With hope, we are compelled to reach far beyond mortal imagination into the realms of miracles perpetuated by faith in God's immeasurable power.

> *"For the grace of God has appeared, bringing salvation for all people, training us to renounce ungodliness and worldly passions, and to live self-controlled, upright, and godly lives in the present age, waiting for our blessed hope, the appearing of the glory of our great God and Savior Jesus Christ, who gave himself for us to redeem us from all lawlessness and to purify for himself a people for his own possession who are zealous for good works."*

TITUS 2:11-14 (ESV)

Grace is God's gift and cannot be earned because it is free, a favor from God. When it appears and we are ready to receive it, transformation occurs, and miraculous events happen. Life changes forever. Let us make a vow that we begin each morning with a prayer to receive fully the amazing grace that is manifested in God's love. Let us imagine ourselves as vessels of divine grace, transforming into the image of Christ, Who died so that we may live to create a world in which persons can live in truth and love.

LESSON 2

Love

I love singing, reading, dancing, watching movies, going thrift store shopping, and eating ice-cream and chocolate. Yet I know my love for these things cannot teach me to love others, nor can they teach me the meaning of God's love. Earthly things such as these limit and confine the meaning of love to self, and in so doing, have us believe we must acquire more in order to feel good. The misconception that the world can fulfill us confuses all that love is because the world is constantly changing, therefore limited in its ability to sustain love. God's love on the other hand is steadfast and unchanging. It is infinite. And infinite love is abundant; it cannot be bought or earned.

God's love, not limited to time or space, encompasses everything and everyone. Spiritual love, freely given, is often rejected simply because it's free. As curator of an antiques business for thirty years, I understand how this works. Many times, I marked down an expensive item to sell it quickly. Even though the item had great value, I noticed people rejected it because of its low price. They didn't perceive the true value based on cost. When receiving God's free gift, we often fail to recognize how valuable His gift is. When we put a price on God's love by doing good deeds, we treat His love as a commodity to be negotiated. We don't realize God's love doesn't have to be earned or purchased. His love is everywhere and dwells within us at all times; we access it with our whole hearts and become vessels for its power. When we find God's love, we, like the man in Matthew, sell everything we have for the treasure in the field. (Matt 13:44-46) We leave behind all we know for the eternal kingdom.

As a little girl I witnessed the opposite of God's love. I witnessed parents fighting bitterly and violently, often taking their anger out on me and my siblings. I have no memory of being held or comforted. Instead of love, I received sarcasm, criticism, and mockery and was physically and psychologically abused. In search of something different, I joined a Christian group called Young Life. During this time of my life, I attended a weekend retreat and enjoyed the freedom of hiking, canoeing, singing, and praying. On the last night of camp, our youth pastor invited us to receive Christ's love into our hearts. He promised our lives would change for the better, and we would feel God's love and mercy. With nothing to lose, I whispered a prayer for God to come into my life. My primary caretakers had betrayed me, and I needed to feel loved. While I prayed, tears began flowing down my face, and I felt God's calm, warm presence cradling me. For the first time in my life, I felt at peace. In the midst of my tears, I heard a soft whisper, "It's going to be alright. I'm with you now." I dwelled in His love and comfort for hours, and by morning I felt emptied of the darkness of anxiety that had so long gripped me. God's divine love, a free gift, had touched and changed me.

Soon I came to rely on God for all my needs. He drove out my fears and gave me courage to face the trials in my life. He taught me about sacrifice, and although I stumbled and fell, He protected me, picked me up, and set me back on track. Most of all, He replaced my earthly mother and father who in their blinding darkness could not care for me in love.

> *"Whoever does God's will is my brother and sister and mother."*
>
> **MARK: 3-35 (NIV)**

I learned that family is not confined to blood relatives. Living in Christ means you have acquired an adopted family who will love and care for you as Christ does. In later years I came to know God's love while working in my garden. I came to understand His relationship to me mirrors my relationships to every living thing. Every living thing needs love in order to grow into its divine potential, and because of our diversity, that looks different for everyone. As I've observed the needs of my beloved plants, I learned that like us, each one is wonderfully distinct from one another and requires individual levels of care. God loves us the same way. He sees what we need in order to grow into His divine love, and He provides it. As Master Gardner of our souls, He tends to His seeds with patience, kindness, and compassion. He does not boast or envy or dishonor us.

> *"...it is not self-seeking it is not easily angered it keeps no record of wrongs.*
>
> **1 CORINTHIANS 13:5 (NIV)**

Unlike the conditional love the world has to offer, God's love endures forever. It wraps our hearts in a blanket of mercy, grace, and truth. It warms and welcomes us into a kingdom of everlasting light and keeps us safe from the perils of darkness. Even when I feel weak or discontented, God loves me. Even though I am not perfect, He loves me. Even though I fail often, He loves me. Love has transformed me and is transforming me still. I am loved, and I am love, because He has bound himself to me, and we are bound together in love. He will never forsake me.

Nothing in this world can replace God's love, yet even though I know this, there are times when I feel distant or disconnected from Him. I know He is there, but I can't feel His presence or His love. Instead of peace, I feel restless and agitated. At these times I pray, read scripture, and ask God to show me the way. I pray for forgiveness for things I have done or left undone. I pray for guidance, healing, and understanding. I read scripture to know Him better as He knows me. Thankfully in His own good time, God reaches out to me in love, and I reach back. I tell Him often how much I love and appreciate Him and thank Him for the wonderful blessings in my life. I don't feel as if I deserve this kind of love, yet He, the infinite source of love, has chosen me. He has chosen you, too. He calls us to love Him with all of our hearts, minds, and souls and to love one another along with ourselves. He calls us home to the love from which we were born. He calls us to give up our worldly loves and seek that which truly nourishes our souls.

God's love, infinite in compassion and redemptive in nature, awakens our souls to a divine life beyond what we could ever imagine. When we receive it, we are called to share it with others so they too will know about the treasure in Heaven that awaits us. God seeks our hearts to come into union with His. He frees us from the bondage of earthly things, so that we may be free to love others in the same way He loves us. God's love lifts us from the lowest valley and sets us on a mountain top where we can shout *Hallelujah!* His love strengthens, encourages, and guides us to peaceful green pastures. His valuable gift is free. Like the Kingdom of Heaven, it is a treasure hidden in the field. When we find it, we must sell all we have to obtain it.

LESSON 3

Servanthood

There are many roles we will play in life, and one of the most important roles I believe, is service to others. Becoming a servant to others opposes our self-serving human nature, yet God gives each of us gifts and asks that we use those gifts in service to others.

> *"As each has received a gift, use it to serve one another, as good stewards of God's varied grace:"*
> **1 PETER 4:10 (ESV)**

In this passage, Peter asks us to serve one another in stewardship according to the grace God has given us. In the name of God's grace, servanthood aims toward the welfare of self, family, neighbors, community, then beyond. If not practiced in our homes first, servanthood becomes a vehicle for self-aggrandizement by serving everyone else—except our closest relationships. How many times have you witnessed a minister, or public servant treat everyone with generosity, goodwill, and grace, yet ignore their spouse and children? Servanthood, the true nature of it, begins with the lessons we teach our children. It begins with how we treat those closest to us, and it also begins with our self. How can we serve others if we have not treated ourselves with love, grace, forgiveness and generosity? How do we help others become healthy and whole if we are not healthy and whole ourselves?

Serving ourselves begins with our relationship with God. It is letting God serve our needs so we can serve others. When we allow God to serve our needs, we in turn can serve our husbands, wives, children, and community. In this way, the family becomes the bedrock for our servant role in society. Today's families may be different from families of the past, but the concept remains the same. If you can imagine a pebble being thrown into water, you will see the ripple effect of that pebble reaching far beyond its limits. When we allow God to be the pebble of our lives, we learn to take care of ourselves so we can take care of our family, then our family learns to serve others, and those others have the capacity to move beyond the smaller circle and serve the world. As God enters our life, His love and service to us creates this ripple effect to our loved ones and beyond.

In another analogy, God tells us that a husband's role toward his wife is like the role of Jesus' servant role to the church. (Ephesians 5:23) If Jesus were not available to inspire, instruct, and invite us into the ways of love and servanthood, the church would lose its way and be unavailable to serve the needs of others; likewise, with a husband toward his wife. The wife or woman is a vessel to be filled; when she is not, like the church, her ability to love and serve others becomes stunted. Becoming like Jesus in our families is a choice. God gives us the choice to mirror Him or not. It is our choice to serve God, our spouses, our children, and others with love, respect, kindness, and generosity. This act of free will never implies obligation.

> *"You, my brothers and sisters, were called to be free. But do not use your freedom to indulge the flesh; rather serve one another humbly in love."*
>
> **GALATIANS 5:13 (NIV)**

Along with the servant role of husband to wife and vice-versa, one of the more difficult roles of servanthood in society is that of a parent to a child. As parents adapt to their newborn child, their commitment to serving the child's needs is paramount to the welfare of society at large. A good parent sees their duty to their child as one of self-sacrifice in order to nurture, love, and protect their young. This difficult role requires balancing the needs of the adult with that of the child. Too much sacrifice, the child may become spoiled or selfish; too little sacrifice, and the child may end up with developmental issues. The struggle and strife of this challenging endeavor becomes even more difficult when a child suffers with mental or physical illness. The community's or church's supportive role in raising children then becomes part of community service. Parents need good support. They need resources to help them fulfill the difficult role of parenting, resources such as relatives, friends, and others from the larger community, who help fortify the parents' will, strength, and determination to succeed. In this way, the whole community takes on the servant's heart of God by serving one another. The act of servanthood, like the roles of husband and wife, becomes reciprocal. When parents raise healthy children with the help of community, society gains a productive, giving adult, who in turn serves others.

Still there are many mothers and fathers who do their best to raise children with little or no resources. I experienced this first hand because I lived in a rural community where there were no resources available to me, nor did I have relatives who lived nearby. I had the overwhelming duty of taking on multifaceted roles. My roles included teacher, guidance counselor, house-cleaner, cook, entrepreneur, business executive, accountant, coach, hairdresser, fashion coordinator, bus driver, and health care provider. Only by the grace of God did I succeed (my children may think otherwise) in this demanding and selfless role. Eventually I found a friend who, like me, was desperate for help. We traded babysitting, which allowed us time to attend to personal needs. Many nights during these trying times, I thought of Mary, the mother of Jesus, and wondered what it was like for her. Did Mary struggle as I did? Did she feel inadequate and worry over things mothers worry about? Out of frustration, did she lose her temper as I did with my children? Or were there times where she wanted to relinquish her servant role and take a vacation to the Bahamas? In spite of the obstacles she faced, her reliance on God's wisdom served her well. She remained faithful to God, submitting to His will while raising Jesus, the young man who would change the course of history for all time.

Submitting ourselves to the Lord as Mary did, allows us to develop a compassionate servant's heart. When we serve each other, God leads us into a place of grace, and supplies our hearts with wisdom, courage, and peace. By praying to be a good servant, God delivers what we need by setting an example of servanthood through Jesus, Who came to serve, not to be served. (Mark, 10:45.)

Husbands and wives often fail in this responsibility to one another and model poor servant roles to their children. Rather than serving each other, they expect to be served. Parents who also struggle in their parenting responsibilities often raise children, who as adults, have a higher risk of becoming a detriment to society. When we do not model to our families God's way of selflessness, respect, trust, love, commitment, and sacrifice, they suffer. And when families suffer, the world suffers.

One does not have to look very far to see the world is in desperate need of servants. Two thirds of the world's children live in poverty and sub-standard housing. Nursing homes are overcrowded and understaffed, and our education system is below standard because the best and the brightest are forced to look for jobs which provide a more substantial income. If we were to spend more time honoring those who serve society by serving others, societies would reveal the love and compassion that God so desperately tries to teach us.

Our faith walk calls upon us to love God, walk in obedience to Him, keep His commands and serve Him with all our heart, mind, and soul. And serving God means serving others. Our purpose is to submit to God, Who loved us so much that He sacrificed His only Son. The example of this kind of selfless love is the love that God wishes for us to demonstrate to others in our lives. A servant of God is not looking for their name to be embossed on a brass plate commemorating their lifelong commitment. A servant of God is seeking to show others the light of our Creator through the selfless act of servanthood. When we spend our lives serving God, we are commissioned as saints to breathe into others the essence of God's hope, faith, and love in order that they too may grow in the light of salvation.

When our human needs are filled through the selfless service acts of others, we in turn are filled with the willing spirit to give back. When aging parents need assistance, we assist; when a neighbor needs a helping hand, we help; and when the local food bank needs food, we give. Along with these roles, we can choose careers that serve the needs of others: doctors, firemen, paramedics, social workers, teachers, ministers, as well as countless volunteer jobs serve the needs of other people, and God does not forget when we serve in ministry to others.

> *"God is not unjust; he will not forget your work and the love you have shown him as you have helped his people and continue to help them."*

HEBREWS 6:10 (NIV)

By serving our loved ones, families, and community, God magnifies our soul as we compassionately serve His people. Serving others with a willing heart and mind fills us with a purpose that nothing in this material world can. By committing ourselves to God and serving Him, we are commissioned to love and serve our families, community, and the world in a way that reflects the heavenly kingdom of God's grace, mercy, and profound love.

CHAPTER 18

"A Time for Peace"

*In the presence of God, nothing stands
Between Him and us- we are forgiven
But we cannot feel his presence
If anything stands between ourselves
and others.*

DAG HAMMARSKJOLD

LESSON 1

Renewal

While visiting with a group of Christian women, I was struck by one who said it was difficult for her to relax and do nothing. She said she felt guilty whenever she rested, knowing more important tasks were at hand. In many ways I could relate to what she was saying. At the time, I ran a business (often working ten hours a day,) coached little league baseball, participated in the PTA, and taught dance at my local church.

My life could be historically documented by the pages of lists I'd written: projects, tasks, grocery lists, and responsibilities. At one time I considered saving all my lists and publishing them as a testimonial to my life. Somehow feeling my self-worth was tied to my accomplishments, I studied how to double up on tasks, as if one task at a time was not productive enough. This frenzied lifestyle left me feeling drained and yearning for something different, but I didn't know how to change. I felt guilty when I rested, just like the woman in my church.

Why, I wondered, *in our culture do we feel guilty if we aren't productive every minute of every hour of every day?* We self-impose our need for accomplishment, accepting super-human demands on our time, without considering the cost to our soul. Dividing our precious time amongst work, family, church, and household tasks, we miss the opportunity to connect with God who gives rest and comfort to our weary hearts.

> *"Come to me all you who are weary and burdened I will give you rest. Take my yoke upon you and learn from me. For I am gentle and humble in heart, and you will find rest for your souls. For my yoke is easy and my burden light."*
>
> MATTHEW 11:28-30 (NIV)

God's yoke is easy, and His burden is light. He believes we are worthy to be loved just as we are, in stillness or activity. He encourages us to rest in Him without guilt or blame. When we realize we are worth being loved and cared for even though we are taking time off, we can relax, and in doing so, discover that we have renewed energy to take care of the tasks at hand. To make new, or *renew*, is *to start again, to refresh oneself or to become strong again.* When we refresh our worn and weary spirits in the loving light of God, we are able to create and generate more love, more care, and more compassion for others. The farmer's relationship to his crops are an example of renewal that comes to mind. Every season, farmers rotate their crops allowing for the renewal of the soil. If they didn't, the produce would be diminished and diseased. They allow one year for the soil to rest and replenish itself, making it more productive over the course of time. Just imagine if you were told to renew yourself for one year. How would you tend to your soul in order to be more vital in the world? In Leviticus 25:1-7, the author speaks about God's directive to Moses. He tells Moses that the land and the people need to rest for a year, following six years of labor.

Unfortunately, today we are not farmers, so it is not likely that we would take a year off, but God does instruct us to take time to renew ourselves weekly by remembering the Sabbath and keeping it holy. In both Genesis 2:3 and Exodus 20:8-11 God directs us to rest and recognize Him as our spiritual life-force. This practice of rest is carried out in the traditional Jewish Sabbath, which is practiced every Friday to Saturday evening. The preparations begin as early as Friday morning. Prior to the evening ritual, chores and meals are completed before sundown. White linen tablecloths, glowing candles, freshly baked Hallah bread, and songs or prayers are hallmarks to this ancient tradition. For the next twenty-four hours no work of any kind is allowed. Instead, the primary focus includes reading, relaxation, and family togetherness, including games, singing, or reading the Torah. In contrast, the Western Sunday "Day of Rest" (as I have experienced it), includes a harried ritual of rushing through breakfast, scrambling to get to church on time, cooking and cleaning after Sunday dinner, and a mad dash to oversee homework and prepare school clothes for the next day.

This common scenario experienced by many Americans is considered a day of rest and woefully reflects the Sabbath of the Jewish tradition. God intends for us to rest and relax each week. God, the Healer of our souls gives us the prescription to be still in the midst of our hurried lives. (Psalm 46:10a) He tells us to study His Word and rest in His presence. He counsels through His own experience of creation, and advises it is wise to refurbish our weary souls after a long week of labor. I wonder how many illnesses would be prevented or cured if doctors handed this out as a prescription? If the supreme sovereign King of creation takes time to rest, why don't we make time to do the same? What is compelling us to accept the madness of sixty-hour work weeks with little or no time for God or our families? Could it be that we don't trust in God's provision, believing instead in our over-achieving, over-indulgent, Ego-driven nature?

God does not worry about what we can produce or procure. He is interested in our souls and warns us that rust and moth will eventually destroy our material possessions, so it is prudent not to put too much stock in them. (Matt. 6:20) He wants our souls to become fertile ground for the divine seed He planted in us, and we can do this if we take time to renew our hearts, minds, and bodies with the rich nutrients of God's Word, healthy food, exercise and rest. Resting in God allows us to renew and reboot which brings more strength, more energy, and more focus to our lives.

God's divine plan includes sitting still with Him

and listening with our hearts. When we do, we feel the depth of peace that passes all understanding and come to know God as a loving Shepherd who watches over His flock. No longer do we have to work until exhaustion because we've allowed God to take over.

God calls us to come to Him into a quiet place and rest. He tells us that His yoke is not heavy, and His burden light. If we are still, we may hear Him calling us to come home and rest in His arms, while He wraps us in a blanket of love and acceptance. We may even decide that taking time off to be with God is the best investment we will ever make!

Inch by Inch

When traveling on God's road, we often move in directions we did not originally intend to go. For myself, plotting the path to my spiritual destiny seems slow and arduous, and I wonder if I'm going in the right direction. Still, there are those who make their way to the divine garden where they spend hours meditating and cultivating a spiritual life. In either situation the spiritual journey can trudge along at a snail's pace. While learning to conform to God's will, we inch along in our journey and wait for enlightenment to come. And when it does, we begin to get a glimpse of the budding life of divine light that when nurtured and cared for cannot falter in the face of adversity.

The journey is marked with passion as well as pain, and as we're enlightened, we come to realize the journey has no real end because the spiritual life is a continuum of slowly allowing ourselves to be perfected into the image of God so we may enter eternal life. Of course, there are moments of great triumph, when our spiritual enthusiasm glows with the embers of the Holy Spirit, and we feel the sensation that every planet in the universe is aligning itself to the beat of our heart. But more often than not, we feel stuck, bogged down, and sidetracked as we inch along in the muddy realities of earthly life. Just when events start to align themselves, something near catastrophic shatters our confidence and plunges us back into the dark depths of spiritual doubt. This aggravating occurrence is not accidental as it reminds us that we have not yet learned our lessons and must continue with perseverance, the slow process of learning and practicing the lessons of the divine.

We must not be hard on ourselves because even those who were closest to Jesus had many doubts and setbacks. His own brother Mark did not believe in Him, and His disciple Thomas had apprehensions as well. Eventually all those closest to Christ became unwavering in their belief and spent the rest of their lives evangelizing and risking their lives to ensure the continuance of the faith. The impact that Jesus had on them was life altering, and because of that, two thousand years later, disciples are still spreading the word.

The destination on our spiritual journey is not nearly as important as each step we take on our pathway to salvation. God's vested interest in our spiritual maturity and growth compares to the patience of a vintner waiting for a fine wine to mature. Slowly and surely our faith becomes steady and unwavering as we drench ourselves in the wisdom of God's Word. If we rush, we might miss opportunities to learn about the love that God has so graciously planted along our path. The obstacles and set-backs that seem to hinder us are really God's way of forcing us to slow down and experience the truth about life from a divine perspective. Anyone who believes, can attest to this, as it can best be described as a feeling of heavenly enlightenment mixed with earthly anxiety.

There are many examples in my life of this strange combination of earthly and divine emotions, but the one that I recall most vividly entails the remodeling of my house. Many years ago, I refinanced my home to enlarge the cramped living conditions. The project included a complete kitchen remodel and a modest addition. I spent many painstaking hours planning, drawing, and measuring each inch of the house. I made sure I was not overlooking possibilities for improvement. I made hundreds of trips to Home Depot to price and compare products. I interviewed as many as twenty construction workers, including concrete workers, electricians, framers, dry wall contractors, roofers, and various handymen. Enthusiastic and energetic, I kept a fresh vision of how beautiful the project was going to eventually look. But the process quickly began to crawl at a painstakingly slow pace, and I grew tired and weary with each roadblock. Every time unforeseen problems arose, weeks were added onto the projected timetable and my fresh vision began to turn stale.

At the same time as the remodel, God presented two foreign exchange students who had been mistreated by their original families and had nowhere to go. After much deliberation, we accepted the challenge, but shortly thereafter, my family's patience ran scarce.

Our house overflowed with a Russian, an Israeli, my daughter, son, husband, myself, dog BoBo, and cat Lilly. Not only were the six of us cramped in our living space, there was a constant barrage of construction workers coming and going at all hours. Between us, we shared one bathroom, three bedrooms, a small living room, and a construction site for a kitchen.

As I look back on the experience, I see God's hand in the project. He showed me the truth about life and what is really important. The project took many months and seemed as if it would never end, yet some of my most cherished memories were hidden in that arduous journey. I remember the day we poured the foundation; each one of us read a personal note out loud and placed it in one of the cornerstones. As Thanksgiving drew near, we constructed a make-shift table out of plywood and saw-horses and placed it in the unfinished addition. The large empty space provided a place for games and dancing during the Christmas holiday, and the kids hung like monkeys from the open rafters. I took multiple photographs and sent them to the students who left before it's completion. The earthly distractions and troubles soon faded and the memories of our beautiful exchange students and the experiences we shared remained. God let me know in no uncertain terms, the jewels hidden in life are in the small moments and relationships we experience along the way.

Along the spiritual journey we often question why the outcome did not go as planned, yet we fail to see, hidden amongst the obstacles, the messages of God's love. Contained in these messages are God's truth. These messages are paramount to learning to grow in the light of the Spirit. For me the lesson was learning that within four walls, love is not subject to timelines and completion dates. Through God's diversions and roadblocks, we slowly learn to accept and embrace our human impatience with ourselves, as well as others' as part of our condition on earth. Our slow inch-by-inch spiritual growth teaches us that the spiritual life is a journey not a destination. We grow and develop our character slowly as we are mirror the reflection of God's love, a love that overcomes death, as well as housing remodels!

LESSON 3

The Journey

From the time I turned fifteen and asked Jesus into my life, I unknowingly embarked on a lifelong journey of faith. Along the way, the mountains and valleys of life taught me much about how God works. Suffering taught me more about myself than my mountain top experiences, and sometimes I suffered repeatedly until I learned my lesson. Of all the things I've learned, the most important message was discovering the divine purpose of learning to know, love, and trust a loving and peaceful God, Who continues to teach me about myself in relationship to others. As I come to know and grow in the likeness of God, more questions reveal themselves to me. Should I set aside my needs for the needs of others, or serve myself? Or another question challenges me whether to indulge in earthly treasures which rot and rust, or spend valuable time and money helping family, friends, and strangers.

In both cases, I found myself struggling with my earthly desires versus the need for connection with others. I eventually came to the conclusion that selflessness has more virtue than selfishness, and landfills are overflowing, so why continue to consume goods that do not last? Ultimately, I came to the decision that balance between self and others proves essential to fulfilling a Godly life. If you look at scripture, God tells us to love others as we love ourselves. If we are not loving and kind and giving to ourselves, we will not have the capacity to love and give to others. To understand this has taken me a long time, but the journey has been worth it.

Because God is relational, He wants to have a relationship with us so that we may experience His peace in all our interactions. Loving God with our whole heart, mind, and soul helps us do this. In so doing, I have experienced that whatever proves necessary to foster God's peace inevitably leads me on a journey of the heart. The heart-journey takes me through life, death, joy, sorrow, hope, and despair, which are inescapable experiences that all humanity shares. If we ask the question as did the Pharisees, as to which is the greatest commandment of all we would get the same answer: "...Love the Lord your God with all your heart and with all your soul and with all your mind. This is the first and greatest commandment. And the second is like it: "Love your neighbor as yourself." Matthew 22:37-39 (NIV)

Through shared experiences I find common ground and compassion with others. And I've learned that nothing separates me from another unless I foster it. By living out these two commandments I can understand and appreciate how God sees everyone equally through the light of love, a lens which sees only good in others. My journey and call to ministry help me to view others in this same light. Though seeing like God proves difficult, the effort to learn and practice peace is worthwhile. Whether difficult or easy, this endeavor becomes fertile ground for practicing my faith. God's people at their best bind together in this peace-filled faith-practice. They, like millions of raindrops with a singular divine purpose, saturate and quench dry souls with the love of Jesus. God's people at their best fulfill their calling by treating others with equal respect, attention, love, forgiveness and grace.

The gifts we have been given by God help us to fulfill this divine purpose. We are called in different ways to unite and help others. While some of us are called to accomplish great feats of valor and bravery, others are called to simplicity and prayer. And though we may not fully understand the mystery of God's calling, when looking back, we understand and acknowledge His wisdom in our lives. I have often envisioned God's mystery like a dot-to-dot picture, the kind we had in coloring books as children. The random dots we see mark all the experiences in our lives which sometimes seem to have no meaning or purpose. Yet when looking back, we connect the dots and see the journey with all its twists and turns laid out before us. Then we see clearly the relationships and connections we've made coming together to create a beautiful image that reveals God's love, will, peace and grace. Though more often than not we are led astray by our stubborn ego and zealous determination, the faith-journey nudges us gently and redirects us back to the garden where it all began. The journey takes us back to Eden where we fell from grace; it teaches us the forgiveness of God and the lessons of redemption.

On this journey, with all our failures, God constantly calls us home where we rediscover ourselves in the light of His love. My favorite movie of all time is *The Wizard of Oz*, when Dorothy went looking for her heart's desire, she learned in the end that it was right in her own backyard. She learned that her family, friends, and farm were her Eden, for she felt safe and loved there. When we get lost like Dorothy and go looking for something, God often leads us back home to the garden of our youth, or the home we remember as a child. Although for some it may be painful, our childhood home on earth, and all its struggles, remain the center of who we are and where we came from. Because God doesn't make mistakes, we become whole by embracing our history and allowing God to use our story to help others. Everyone has a story to tell, a story that could play an important role in furthering God's Kingdom. What we may view as darkness in our childhood God transforms into light. "Even the darkness will not be dark to you; the night will shine like the day, for darkness is as light to you." Psalm 139:12 (NIV)

God sees no darkness only light, and the divine destiny and purpose of our lives may in fact reside or be born in the darkness that we have suffered. When we allow the Great Healer, who sees only light, to come into our lives, we are delivered from darkness and sin. This redemption allows the light of God to shine in every corner of our being. And when we are filled with the light, it radiates beyond us to others who need healing. This is why we should remember the assertion made by Jesus that is recorded in the Gospel of John: "Truly, truly, I say to you, whoever believes in me will also do the works that I do; and greater works that these will he do, because I am going to the Father." John 14:12 (ESV) This calling and responsibility, when answered wholeheartedly, leads us to fulfilling our purpose, God's purpose to bring light and peace to the world.

Often in life we will be called by God. When we answer *Yes, Lord!* our faith journey begins. My calling came at a Young Life camp in Arizona. There I chose to ask God into my life. In the hour of my need, He delivered, and my healing began. You have the choice, just as I did, to accept the invitation to a life in Christ, a life with God who heals, comforts, counsels, protects, and offers grace and forgiveness. But no matter what, it is always a choice to accept God's invitation because He is a God of free will, not oppression. Made in the image of God, we are called to find our way back to Godliness. And if we can, in our short time on earth, accomplish what God has lovingly laid out for us, we will win another small battle in the great war against darkness.

After accepting the invitation, we must also accept that like Jesus' journey, all of our journeys on earth must come to an end. But through the resurrection, our souls live on in eternity as well as in the hearts and minds of men, women, and children whom we have loved along the way. Our seed, God's seed, planted in us at birth, takes a lifetime to blossom. When nurtured, loved, and watered with God's Word, our "soul-seed" grows and eventually withers. But before it does, God's seeds, like those of a flower or tree, are spread to others with the hope of expanding the Divine Kingdom. The divine seeds we sow with love have the opportunity to bloom into new life in Christ. In so doing, love is regenerated, hope is renewed, and joy abounds. Finally, in the end we may rejoice in knowing, "He will wipe every tear from their eyes. There will be no more death or mourning or crying or pain, for the old order of things has passed away." Revelation 21:4 (NIV)

ABOUT THE AUTHOR

 Cathy Gregory lives with her husband Russell in Flower Mound, Texas, along with her rescue dog Pippi and fat cat Lilly. She has served joyfully as a liturgical dance minister for over 16 years at various churches in Texas. Having done mission work in both New Orleans and Puerto Rico, Cathy continues to look for ways to serve around the world by helping others in their time of need. In her spare time Cathy paints, dances, and spends time with her grown children, Libby and Spencer, and her grandchild, Miles.

WEBSITE
http://cathylynngregory.com/

Made in the USA
Coppell, TX
14 July 2020

30885078R00135